PowerSkills

PowerSkills

BUILDING TOP-LEVEL
RELATIONSHIPS FOR
BOTTOM-LINE RESULTS

JAMES P. MASCIARELLI

Nimbus Press, Gloucester, Massachusetts

Published by Nimbus Press
84 Main Street, Gloucester, MA 01930

Publishers Cataloging-in-Publication
(Provided by Quality Books, Inc.)

1 2 3 4 5 6 7 8 9 10

Masciarelli, James P.
    PowerSkills: building top-level relationships
for bottom-line results/James P. Masciarelli —
1st ed.
    p. cm.
Includes bibliographical references and index.
LCCN: 99-69863
ISBN: 0-9677111-1-8

    1. Success in business. 2. Interpersonal
relations. 3. Organizational effectiveness.
4. Relationship marketing. I. Title

HF5386.M37 2000   650.1'3
                                   QBI99-1936

Cover & Interior Design: Laura Herrmann Design

TO MY PARENTS

This book is dedicated to my parents, Adeline and Rocco, whose 62 years of marriage have been an inspiration for me.

My mom "Addie" is the greatest relationship manager I have ever known, and my Dad "Rocky" the most unselfish and disciplined taskmaster I have ever had as a role model.

Thanks to both of them, I have spent my life trying to best balance my own life's relationships and tasks according to their high standards.

CONTENTS

PREFACE

This book has been and continues to be a journey for me. I sincerely hope you will enjoy and act upon the insights compiled within its pages. Although as this book's author, I must take modest credit for presenting the ideas described here, these are ideas that have in fact taken centuries to evolve. What is new in this book, however, is a framework for daily action from lessons learned from great leaders of history and refined by current-day heroes in the workplace.

This project began in 1994 as I contemplated a professional shift into executive and organizational development. During this period of contemplation, I began to catalog the lessons I had learned from some of the best and brightest executives, entrepreneurs, managers, business owners, and professionals with whom I had had the pleasure to work. My "border-crossing" past provided a context—first as a director of social work, then a corporate human resource executive, next as a retained high-tech executive search consultant, president of two service companies and, finally, as board member and private investor.

I wanted to capture some of my hard-won experiences for the benefit of other business leaders and help those with ambitions to create or grow their own businesses or capabilities. I also wanted to share some fundamentals of business success that could benefit those in the beginning or intermediate stages of their professional work life. This is a period for most of us when we could truly use such solid "success principles" when we haven't yet experienced enough hard knocks to have acquired them on our own.

As a corporate and retained executive search consultant, I had interviewed more than 10,000 executives face-to-face over a 22-year period. As I observed, probed, and referenced how careers unfolded, the critical factors for the success of business leaders became evident to me in a way that wasn't being written about. From listening many times to real business success stories I gained a key insight into what long-term business success was all about—the building, leveraging, and nurturing of a strategic web of professional relationships.

The more I probed, the more I confirmed that this dynamic went far beyond the notion of networking. It was instead the development of a strategic value-producing asset that crossed many boundaries in many meaningful ways. I have since come to conceptualize the skills and methods I had seen others wield, to powerful advantage, as the "PowerSkills" of managing professional relationships.

A second insight was that business leaders usually develop these skills through trial and error over many years and are unaware of how to translate them into frameworks others can easily learn. During moments of frustration with their peers, coworkers, and subordinates, such leaders often make the mistake of taking their own priceless skillset as a given, expecting others to "just do it." I concluded that an effective learning framework that could be taught, observed, and practiced was badly needed.

To develop a framework for building successful relationships required going well beyond the purview of most business texts and business courses. Relationship Management (RM) is truly both art and science. Having said this, I found that the scope of my work in this broad area came to focus upon how real business value is created through collaboration.

In my attempt to intricately understand the nuances of this area, I have delved into the fields of psychology, personality theory, self development, leadership, sales methodologies, marketing theory and practice, relationship marketing, database marketing, communications, and new media management practices. I also reviewed the writings of sages and philosophers that deeply considered relationships. My challenge was to figure out how to integrate these fields of study with my business experience and produce a practical and jargon-free framework that can transform the work habits of individuals, teams, and organizations. My goal is to share a few keen observations and meaningful generalizations that business leaders of today (and tomorrow) can apply in practical and profitable ways.

Although many of the concepts in this book could be considered timeless, the book is also written from the viewpoint of today's workplace, with its globalization, flatter organizations, outsourcing, playing fields of "free agents," pervasive information networks, and new technology tools to be mastered. In this often-overwhelming environment, one could say that we have become, in the way our business is conducted, "technology-rich" while "relationship-poor." It is also clear that we have entered a "paradox of empowerment" period in which people are made power-full by technology, yet feel increasingly power-less by what seems to be unworkable organizational designs. In such a context, the greatest surprise can be that decisions are made at all.

PowerSkills can help us to empower ourselves. It can help us to begin building bridges that many of today's organizations do not, and perhaps should not, provide for us. Power, after all, is that unique quality that results from the formation and management of our relationships. Power which affords an individual or group the ability to initiate, manage, direct, control, and even resist change. It is a brave new world, and to be brave in it, one needs effective PowerSkills to survive, thrive, and transcend the ordinary.

On any given day, we do well or poorly as a result of the dimensions of our personal leadership skills. Yet our personal leadership can, and must, be applied to self-management, project management, and relationship management, spurring us to do what good leaders do: think, plan and relate. Though this book is primarily about relating strategically, more importantly it is about *mastering* relationships and incorporating them as a way of life.

As has been true for my own process while researching and writing this book, I can assure you that mastering relationships is a life-long journey.

INTRODUCTION

CASE 1: JOHN RILEY

At the age of 39, John Riley became a multi-millionaire when the 42-person venture-backed software company he ran as Chief Executive Officer (CEO) was acquired by one of the fastest-growing high-technology public companies in the world. Today John is a General Manager with that organization and, as a result, has an opportunity to fundamentally change the way people use computing systems.

John's accomplishment in readying his start-up company for sale was significant. Joining originally as Vice President (VP) of Sales, he quickly learned that his new employer's technology and product positioning was far from optimal. In fact, the venture capitalists on the company's board were unsure themselves if the company could make it. As a result, they'd become more and more reluctant to continue funding the effort. Their idea was to put John in charge as top officer temporarily, until they could figure out what else to do.

John took it from there. Not only did he prove to be a brilliant leader internally, he began forging dynamic partnerships outside the company as well, leveraging and expanding its value. In the end, he successfully raised badly needed capital, put together a whole new management team, added an advisory board, and found new ways to retain the company's brightest employees. Overall, he vanquished a pervasive negative thinking that had been festering within the company, turning attitudes around and pointing the team in a new, and prosperous, direction.

How could a young, first-time, non-technical CEO assume the helm of such a demoralized, dysfunctional, misguided technical organization and take it to stunning victory in less than two years?

John Riley had discovered a secret formula.

CASE 2: MARY ERIKSON

Mary Erickson came to the United States as a college graduate in Liberal Arts from a northern European country. Just married to Dan, an American who had recently completed his junior year abroad at her university, Mary knew not one soul in America. But as an engineer poorly versed in people skills, Dan had little to offer Mary when it came to helping her get her young career off the ground. Mary became resigned early on to advancing her skills all by herself.

And Mary had much to overcome, personality-wise. Though petite and, at first glance, demure, she was in fact a scrapper who could suddenly become brash. It didn't help that a thick foreign accent often made her difficult to understand. On the plus side, she was a quick learner, extremely bright, and an energetic, enthusiastic risk-taker. Behind her impatient, feisty demeanor lay a heart of gold and a fearsome integrity that only those few souls who really knew her ever got to see.

Where is Mary today? She's a Vice President with a Fortune 500 organization, listed as one of the "Best Companies to Work for in America." She previously worked for several companies in different industries in both senior line and staff roles; her career moves are all expertly timed, solid professional accomplishments. She's been a mentor to both women and men attempting to advance their own careers over the years and has earned the respect not only of her peers but of every CEO she has ever worked for. At this point in her professional life, people in three different industries know her to be the truly talented high-achiever she so obviously is.

With all her initial disadvantages, how did Mary shoot so rapidly to the top, smashing through the glass ceiling and piling up brilliant personal achievements (two children raised and a fine golf swing) to go along with her professional ones?

Mary had also acquired a powerful secret.

CASE 3: FRANK RICHARDS

An engineer who became Vice President of Research & Development (R&D) for a major capital equipment company at a very young age, Frank Richards ultimately broke away, in his mid-30s, to found his own manufacturing company. He went on to run this upstart company as its CEO and kept on pushing until it hit the billion-dollar mark. Now Frank's firm is nationally known for fabulous customer service and for the highest quality products. Because of its great reputation, Frank's organization has attracted some of the industry's very best talent.

But Frank's success never went to his head. A lifelong learner and an unpretentious guy, today he serves on several company and not-for-profit boards and enjoys many free-time pursuits including aviation, motorcycling, and outdoor sports. He is the type of leader who can successfully inspire engineering teams and also has a knack for making his company's investors feel secure that their investment is well placed. To the unsuspecting bystander, Frank looks like the kind of natural-born leader who can do it all.

Frank would tell you, however, that he has never done any of it alone. He once remarked to a reporter that the key to business success lies in bringing together a terrific top-flight team, devising a unique product strategy early on and proceeding to implement just the right moves—along with a fair amount of prepared opportunism.

Of all of this, what ingredient would Frank rank highest? When you got him alone, Frank loved to reveal it.

CASE 4: SHARON EVERSON

In over a decade of running her successful graphic design business, Sharon Everson has made only one sales call. That was to the modest local hospital twelve years ago where she got her start. Never a fan of selling, Sharon built a flourishing solo practice that includes the largest companies in her area as well as many small ones. She typically handles high-priority projects such as annual reports, high-gloss marketing brochures and product specifications literature. She loves her work, is very busy and all her clients—all of them!—come to her, not her to them.

Since that initial sales call, business for Sharon has grown strictly through word of mouth. In fact she frequently finds herself turning business away. By completing her assignments through a network of other graphic artists, writers, printers, and designers, and keeping her clientele serviced and herself always aware of their needs, Sharon keeps her operation running seamlessly.

How has she done it? In a field in which lack of loyalty to vendors is the norm, Sharon somehow maintains a solid client list and keeps each customer coming back to her, project after project, year after year. What has made her so successful in gaining referrals and testimonials without even asking?

An event in Sharon's life, in the early years of her business, had transformed her perspective, though it would take many more years for Sharon to realize just how valuable this change would be.

THE KEYS TO SUCCESS FOR EACH

As different as each of these leading professionals are, what do John, Mary, Frank and Sharon have in common? Having known each of these disguised personalities over many years, I can attest that, like many, many other successful professionals I have known, each harbors a commitment for *developing skills that enable them to form relationships to fulfill their dreams.* In the process, they have broken through "relationship blocks" that in younger days had continually gotten in their way.

As a young adult, John Riley developed a penchant for both giving and receiving straight feedback. Over the course of his career he further developed this proclivity, acquiring along the way excellent coaching skills while perfecting a talent for putting good people together to create a whole greater than the sum of all of the pieces. Those practices would eventually make him a great success, forging partnerships that would lead to building a successful company and knowing how to lead so that the company could thrive internally.

Mary Erickson also had improved her ability to listen to other people. Earlier she tended to fly off the handle whenever she believed another was wrong (and that she was right), holding fast a belief in brutal honesty, even when her listener felt demeaned by the process. "Everyone should know where I stand," was Mary's motto.

One day a supervisor explained to her why she was getting passed over for a promotion: "Management doesn't feel you can work well with people and this job requires excellent people skills." Excellent people skills, Mary thought. The words haunted her night and day, for weeks. In the end, she had to admit she didn't really know what they meant.

Determined to find out, Mary began talking with colleagues, her supervisor—anyone who would listen. Excellent people skills, she asked everyone—what do *you* take these words to mean?

By listening hard, forcing herself to hear other points of view, Mary came to see there were usually two sides to every issue. Slowly, her openness to the "other" side began making her professional life much easier. The brashness in check, her communications improved, and people began to feel they worked well with her. In time, professional advancement came her way and kept coming as her newfound skills expanded her network and solidified the loyalty of allies in every walk of her professional life.

For Frank Richards the key had been an ability to lift his head above the details and take a good look at real people. For years, he had thought that things, in the world of work, were more important than people, and that colleagues and customers would come and go but that ideas, embodied in a company's products, held the most durable value. As the rate of technological change picked up in the 90s, Frank had a change of heart. Retaining real people—customers and employees alike—was the real ticket, he realized. If you could serve customers on a level that made them feel special, they'd stay with you, even when your products failed to keep pace, as they inevitably must in an age fraught with swift and frequent change. On the other end, by treating employees as if *they* were special, they would stay with you too, continuing to pump out great ideas for new products that would keep your customers happy and save the day.

Although Frank had always understood that no one makes it through alone, these insights accelerated his relationship-building. He developed habits like giving credit to others when appropriate and making sure teams had resources they needed, space to create, and continual challenges to keep them growing. Teamwork became Frank's middle name and nurturing and maintaining relationships his competitive advantage.

Growing up in a broken home, Sharon Everson never knew her real father. A shy child, she had moved with her mother 23 times by the time she was twenty. The many moves did nothing to raise her self-confidence and so she kept apart from people whenever she could, a genuine loner.

In her early thirties she married an entrepreneur named Peter who took special interest in her professional development, encouraging her to think and act outside her comfort zone. One day, she enrolled in a desktop publishing course, picking up its principles so well that the school's administration asked her to *teach* the same course the next semester! Though terrified to take them up on this offer, with encouragement and coaching from Peter, she went forward, blossoming during the next several years, teaching first the basic class, then adding several more advanced courses as well.

This experience of getting up in front of a class buoyed her self-confidence to a level, enhancing her skills in interacting, communicating, negotiating—you name it! Working with so many different kinds of people in each class, coaching them, clarifying assignments for them, setting boundaries—all could be applied to her business affairs and relationships with customers, vendors, and business partners.

Today, she attributes her success to the relationship management skillset she developed while leading her classes and which she began practicing in daily life. Keeping her customers informed of her progress on projects, she takes care to never forget the high value of frequent and clear communication. Where once she might have defined work as a series of tasks, she now sees that true success lies in completing tasks *and* in initiating, facilitating, and sustaining her professional relationships.

BUILDING RELATIONSHIPS IN YOUR OWN CAREER

The central theme of this book is well illustrated by the sagas of John, Mary, Frank, and Sharon. Quite simply, building effective and profitable bottom-line relationships provides a cornerstone for success in today's business world.

Ask any successful business leader in mid-career, or later, what they continue to enjoy most from their careers. They will tell you: it's the satisfaction from collaborations in win-win relationships that have gotten them through it all. I once spoke with Alan Weiss, author of *Million Dollar Consulting* and a prolific writer, speaker, and management consultant, about this issue:

"Alan," I asked him, "you've had a very successful career. What, if anything, would you have done differently to have achieved it all earlier?" His response was instantaneous: "I would have taken care to do a better job of tracking and staying in touch with the outstanding people I have met in my life."

This echoes a common refrain from participants of my seminar programs: "I wish I had developed a more proactive, systematic approach to building relationships like this twenty years ago."

Others have commented: "Paying attention to your relationships broadens your perspective. It starts by asking questions you wouldn't have asked otherwise, and you begin making new connections and coming to better conclusions. In the end, most of these new connections and ideas yield unexpected value."

Another comment: "We need to be reminded from time to time to search for common ground with others. Whenever I forget to do this, I end up conducting business much too narrowly. This limits what I can achieve, and I always pay a heavy price for it."

Have you been sensing similar pain about your own professional skillset? Do you often find yourself regretting you didn't make certain kinds of significant inroads earlier, wincing at the recollection of opportunities lost when you failed to pay attention to someone who could have really helped you—and who *wanted* to help you?

If so, my question to you now is: Why wait one moment longer to change your life?

What's been lacking in business schools and business literature has been a methodology for building webs of strategic relationships that can impact our professions and organizations. Over the last 25 years, I have observed again and again, how applying a balanced set of relationship-building skills can unblock the barricades to true long-term success. Mastering relationships isn't rocket science, but it's arguably more enigmatic and challenging to reduce to formulae. The central essence of success—mastering relationships—is richly multidimensional and builds upon a foundation of first principles. As any accomplished business leader will readily tell you, relationships determine best results.

Even acclaimed success experts such as Tony Robbins typically miss the mark here. In his 400-plus-page best seller, *Awakening the Giant Within,* only four pages are devoted to relationship building! While self-affirmations and other pumping-up techniques can prove useful on a personal level, they are not relational and rarely by themselves deliver a practical plan to reach the larger vision.

BUILDING POWERSKILLS

Relationships in business are pure magic. Build the right ones, integrate, and apply them, and they become assets, blends of synergy and momentum for individuals, teams, and companies. The book you are reading right now defines for you the five fundamental skills that will empower you, to amazing advantage, in your business life, and in your personal life. For that reason, I refer to them as PowerSkills.

In their simplest description, the five basic PowerSkills are:

1. **POSITIONING**—Clearly establishing credibility, desired image, added value, share-of-mind, and strategic intent. Enables you to move your ideas quickly through an organization or network.

2. **HUNTING**—Building the right relationships and obtaining relevant business intelligence. Enables you to recruit your resources and access influencers.

3. **COACHING**—Creating learning relationships and exchanging

extraordinary value on a personal level. Enables you to accelerate learning and become a center of influence.

4. **LEADING**—Practicing closed-loop delegation to obtain desired results from others. Enables you to manage by influence and shape the agenda for change.

5. **FARMING**—Staying connected through nurturing, maintaining and deepening your key relationships. Enables you to strengthen points of customer and client contact.

Throughout this book, I will consider you to be a business leader, whether you are a CEO, business owner, manager, front-line professional, or just a student of business. Your title is less relevant than your attitude. Managing relationships with a leadership mindset will serve you well in any capacity—guaranteed. It is my belief that if each of us gets interactively involved in a community of business leaders with whom we can share our insights, we will add to a definitive body of business relationship knowledge and we will all be the better for it.

To initiate such knowledge expansion, this book contains three distinct parts.

▲ **PART 1:** Provides potent reasons and motivation for a personal commitment to develop the PowerSkills. Part 1 also lays theoretical and analytical foundations for the five PowerSkills, setting out a context for utilizing them all.

▲ **PART 2:** Describes how to apply the overall PowerSkills system, including a detailed description of how each applied skill might affect your life and work. This part of the book can serve as a reference guide for your PowerSkills growth. Suggested exercises and checklists are provided to put your skills to work. You may enter your actions and insights into a PowerSkills journal to track your growth and reinforce your learning.

▲ **PART 3:** Aimed specifically at executives, managers, and team leaders, this section will be useful to those charged with bringing about dramatic improvements in company growth and performance. Here the book will show you how to implement PowerSkills to create high-performance, customer-aligned organizations.

There is also a reference chapter in Part 3 on technologies that can extend and support the application of your developing PowerSkills. Since this material requires constant revision as new technologies emerge, please note that our Powerskills.com website will be available to you with the latest information and links to resources. You need not wait for revised editions of this book to upgrade this information.

Learning and practicing PowerSkills can transform our professional lives, our business organizations, and our personal lives in a positive way.

A larger good will also emerge from spreading the word about PowerSkills, a greater benefit that I believe the world sorely needs. By practicing effective relationship management, we can together put the human touch back in business.

PowerSkills.com

The website www.powerskills.com welcomes your comments, input, stories, lessons learned, suggestions and critiques. The website contains useful resources and links to expand your understanding of the five PowerSkills and help implement the concepts in this book.

PART 1

RELATIONSHIP

MASTERY

CHAPTER 1

RELATIONSHIP POWER AND THE ENTERPRISE

"If the industrial age was about powerful organizations, this 'knowledge era' is about more powerful individuals."

—**Price Pritchett**

More Power, Scotty! *Stardate 5476: This is Captain James T. Kirk, commander of the USS Enterprise, speaking. The crew of the Enterprise is in high spirits tonight as we celebrate the New Year. However, Mr. Checkov has just alerted me about a troubling signal from Europa in our home galaxy. Our mission to explore new worlds has been temporarily suspended. We must embark now to Europa. Warp Speed, Mr. Sulu!*

As a fan, like so many others, of the original television series Star Trek, I marvel at screenwriter Gene Roddenberry's genius in recreating the classical character of Ulysses, mythic King of ancient Ithaca, in the futuristic context of an age of ultra-technology.

Like Ulysses, who traveled the known world by sea with a skilled but very human crew, Captain Kirk led a diverse, high-powered group of specialists who were more skilled than himself in a variety of disciplines yet similarly prone to human weakness. Like Ulysses, who encountered every manner of contemptible beast the Greek gods could throw at him, in all sorts of bizarre settings, Kirk also happened upon astonishing alien creatures, this time in bewildering extraterrestrial environments.

And like Ulysses, with his boundless talent for creative solution-making, Kirk wrapped himself in a kind of emotional intelligence, continually demonstrating an instinct for sizing up whatever problem lay before him and drawing upon logic, feelings, communication skills, and out-of-the-box thinking to see him through.

Although Ulysses and Jim Kirk both deserve the lion's share of credit for their imaginative problem solving, it was skill at orchestrating the talents of their players that served them best, not merely their authority to command them. Ulysses, for example, could not have put out a Cyclops' eye without his crew braving enormous fear by climbing atop the Big C's shoulders and helping to hoist a heavy smoldering log in the right direction.

Kirk as well counted on Spock, Bones, Uhuru, Scotty, and all the rest to aim phasers, beam down to a dangerous surface, switch bodies with an alien life form (i.e., do a "mind meld") or whatever might be needed, if Kirk so requested it. No mutinies here; the crew of the Enterprise knew that Kirk was first in line to face certain death, square off with an alien hulk mano-a-mano to the finish, or offer himself as sole hostage in exchange for his entire crew. Clearly, the voyages of Ulysses' sailing ship and that of the Starship Enterprise were case studies in trust-based leadership resulting in win-win loyalty and in building the kind of interrelationships that allow a true team to achieve its objectives.

To achieve his own ends Jim Kirk also had to overcome extraordinary odds when the technology of the Enterprise was disabled, a mishap that occurred more often than one had any reason to expect. At such moments, Captain Kirk displayed personal leadership skills based more on his charismatic personality than on his appointed position, and in like fashion his crew demonstrated personal leadership whenever their leader's judgment was altered or impaired.

These factors suggest that the popularity of this TV classic may have derived more from the primacy placed on the principles of human interaction than on either its display of technology or any special effects. For that matter, in many episodes, we actually witness Kirk engaged in a duel of wits with a computer of some kind that is invariably portrayed as incapable of making intuitive, i.e., human judgments.

Like Captain Kirk and the legendary Ulysses, most of us in business today are frequently called upon to "explore new worlds," either by ourselves or in small teams. Communicating more and more through an intricate web of relationships we often find ourselves feeling marooned on what seems like a distant planet, or battered by a huge change taking place (alien force) at warp speed. Our responses, ultimate impact, and feelings of job satisfaction all depend on how we develop and utilize a powerbase of relationships largely of our own making. Fortunately for us, Kirk and Ulysses exemplified skills and traits that can indeed be both learned and modeled. Clearly, these skills—the mastery of relationships—are the basis of our potential powers and results.

ARE WE EMPOWERED YET?

Today, there's endless talk about empowerment and providing employees easy access to corporate resources. Yet few corporate people will tell you that they truly feel empowered. This appears to be the case even in some of the so-called "best" companies. The lack of empowerment is chiefly due to a widespread failure at all levels to recognize the hard implications of dramatic organizational changes that have shaped American business throughout the past ten years. There has also been a great failure on the part of most managers to recognize and embrace this call for empowerment; adding to their resistance is their failure to provide resources or training that would enhance empowerment.

No wonder Dilbert has become so popular today, tapping so well the frustration and cynicism of the American worker. One comic strip, for example, from a few years ago, says it all. Hanging on a cubicle wall, in the middle of a vast row of nondescript cubicles, Dilbert himself peers into the next cubicle and realizes the worker there is a new recruit. "What are ya in for?" asks Dilbert. The analogy to prison life in this one quick question captures the lack of empowerment felt by many in the workplace.

As management work becomes more like professional-service work, where everyone is managing projects for "clients" internally (as well as externally), managers feel more and more that they are *doing* more than *managing*. They can mistakenly associate this daily dynamic with a feeling of non-empowerment. Personal leadership and managing-by-influence is now the prevailing idea, not managing through "title power," or through authority derived from one's job title or position in the pecking order. Apparently, this trend will continue, just as our Captain Kirk clearly draws his power less from his authority as commander and more from the loyalty he inspires in his crew. Ulysses, eons ago, had learned this age-old truth.

With business moving closer and closer to warp speed, informal relationships, more than ever, provide professional "glue" and stability. The use of constructive power and influence within these relationships most accurately determines our ability to attain hoped-for bottom-line results. To be really successful at managing-by-influence and at negotiating today's organizations requires highly developed personal leadership, that is, an attitude of life-long learning plus a set of effective power skills. Let's take a closer look at this notion by examining where power actually resides inside organizations.

THE SOURCE OF POWER

The more efficient and plentiful one's collaborations in this information age, the more impact we can have on our respective playing fields and, as a result, the more money a person might earn. Whether they admit it or not, people value power and influence at work more than they value money. Wielded correctly, the use of power can be a very constructive tool.

But power can have a negative aspect, too. Unfortunately, a great deal of workplace behavior is in the pursuit of power for its own sake, and if the negative aspect of power is allowed to fester, a toxic working environment results. Giving in to power's dark side does nothing, in the end, to get you what you want. We end up burning bridges, possibilities, and opportunities. As an executive I know once put it, "Time wounds all heels."

So what is the real potential of power? How is it best cultivated and solidified?

Power, quite simply, is one's ability to cause an event to happen or not to happen, to get things done (or not). Power is derived from the formation and management of relationships. It can even shape others' perceptions and interpretations of events, leading us in effective directions, pointing the way. Ultimately, power equals control, offering predictability and greater input into decisions. The influencing of decisions is itself the highest state of personal influence. We typically associate power with those individuals who have it whether by virtue of their own charisma or by the delegation or legislation of that power. As happened often in the company of both Captain Kirk and Ulysses, power can also be shared and/or transferred from one person to another.

Everyone instinctively recognizes and respects power, though this does not mean they necessarily approve of it. Likewise, when someone with the power to act refuses to use it, an uncomfortable void results and new dynamics intervene. When a business leader creates the impression he might not use his power, he surrenders it!

The Walt Disney Corporation, back in the late sixties, was a case in point. Following their creative founder's death in 1966, the company nearly passed with him. For two decades, top managers at Disney couldn't conceive of anyone filling Uncle Walt's shoes, so they did relatively little risk-taking with the company. Few innovations were tried, no new initiatives put forth.

As a result, mainstays of American culture, such as Disney's weekly television program, one of the longest running shows in TV history, were canceled and Disneyland, badly in need of revamping, went quickly downhill. By the time Michael Eisner took the reins, in

1984, people had stopped following or caring about the pronouncements of Disney's "leaders."

"People here are dying for leadership," new CEO Eisner said at the time, "and they're dying to get to work. If Walt were still alive and ideas had continued to flow out of his mind, Disney would have had no problem." Lesson: Real power demands real action.

People who have the most power are those who seize it and then employ it constructively. Proper positioning and self-promotion of one's ideas, for example, through informal networks is a very effective power builder. Those who understand this idea also know that strong research skills and the ability to gather business intelligence will enhance both their relationship and position power. They also know that much power can be gained through knowledge and information. Most people, however, carry out this perception either poorly or inappropriately, often because they are not properly trained to do primary research.

Many people will even avoid increasing their power because they are too busy seeking approval. They would rather be loved than be powerful. But sometimes business leaders must settle for being respected and sometimes feared instead of loved. Winning their people's love is usually not in their job descriptions. Winning their respect is!

All power has a source. Narrow sources can be identified, modified, or undermined. A broad power base takes energy to build and maintain but is difficult to topple. It is also a very portable asset. The implications of this for business leaders can be enormous. As life can be very lonely at the top, a broad web of advisory and professional relationships outside the company can make it bearable. It is unhealthy, not to mention unnecessary, for leaders to endure the disappointments and isolation that occur naturally when they rely too much on internal supports. Relationships on the outside will bolster their psychological health, helping them do the job, and affirming their power.

THE POWER OF INFORMAL HUMAN NETWORKS

To be effective, business leaders need to fully understand how power operates in their organizations and in the organizations of their customers. Since today's organizational charts often do not reflect true power structures, or how decisions get made, it is vital to understand the dynamics. Here are a few observations of how power operates inside organizations.

▲ **POWER FLOWS THROUGH INFORMAL HUMAN NETWORKS.** Unlike formal, public, or organizational structures, relationships within informal systems are negotiated as "social contracts" and are personalized in one-to-one communications. These informal human networks fail to tolerate excuses or breeches of confidentiality. They are also extremely successful in getting things accomplished across organizational boundaries. Ultimately, invisible informal systems make both organizations and extra-organizations work.

EXAMPLE: The Internet service provider (ISP) Mindspring outgrew many similar providers in the second half of the nineties. Only the giants of AOL, Compuserve, and Microsoft Network exceeded Mindspring's growth. Yet Mindspring did virtually no advertising nor embarked on any heavy marketing campaign.

The enthusiasm of its customers spread the word like high-tech wildfire, not only over the Web but voice-to-voice and face-to-face. The Mindspring human network, as informal as such things get, made this brand new company a marketplace winner.

▲ TRUE COOPERATION IS NOT FORMALIZED. Informal systems seek to remain private and hidden. The strongest currencies, i.e., vehicles of value exchange, in an informal system are delivering information, introductions, or ideas without taking credit. The informal system becomes harder to stay connected with as you move up the corporate pecking order where power, more formalized there, *depends* on receiving credit. In the informal system, however, do not expect credit to flow your way.

EXAMPLE: Although he never held any formal office, was not a wealthy man or known for any special talents, skills or knowledge, Mohandas (Mahatma) Gandhi is credited with driving the British Empire out of India. How did he do it?

In the beginning, Gandhi spent whatever time he could spare speaking to whoever would listen about the need for Indian independence, the potential benefits, and implications for the future. He also shared his thoughts on the immorality of the British presence in his homeland.

After speaking everywhere he could for some time, Gandhi eventually stopped talking and began walking, specifically from Calcutta to the Indian Ocean. As he walked, an informal human network gathered around him, growing in greater and greater numbers each day to support of his views and stayed by his side until he reached the sea. By the end of his trek, India's newest

leader had acquired such power of numbers that British author-
ities recognized their own power had disappeared and quietly
packed up all their belongings to depart their "possession" for
good. True power—cooperation—is not formalized.

▲ THE GRAPEVINE IS A SOURCE OF POWER. It is worth understanding group dynamics and how opinion is shaped in an
informal system. People tend to create their own informal
grapevines by clustering, generally, in groupings of four to six
(just like grapes). Clusters of four to six are natural work groups
and table sizes. Clusters usually get formed through self-
selection, similarity, or common agendas. Clusters establish,
automatically, their own opinion leaders and interact well with
the rest of the network.

EXAMPLE: We've all observed, in just about every group we've
participated in, that some individuals are quiet and some are not.
Those who are not often become opinion leaders. Those who are
quiet are asked, if the group's leader is alert to the problem,
"Now, Joy (or Ben or Pete or Joan), we haven't heard from you in
a while. What do *you* think about this issue?"

To become an opinion leader in an informal human network,
you must frequently contribute useful, fact-based, analyzed,
and new information. That's it.

THE PURPOSE OF BUSINESS

No discussion of power in business would have relevance without focusing on its desired results. Why indeed does power matter at all in business? What is the purpose of utilizing it in this arena?

Whenever I ask business executives these questions, in the form of their definition of the *purpose* of business, I get lots of interesting—and very different!—answers. Yet this is an important and fundamental question. When such an answer, especially from a top business executive, is poorly formulated and then acted upon, a great deal of misery and confusion results. From that leader's unwritten, ad hoc philosophy are shaped the priorities of the business, often to everyone's great misfortune.

The most common answer I get is "to make money." But I then ask: For whom? After all, breaking and entering a convenience store is also an activity carried out for the purpose of making money, yet this endeavor hardly meets the test of the definition of a sustainable ethical business concern.

Another answer I get is that the purpose of business is "to satisfy customers," sometimes followed by the age-old wise refrain, "After all, the customer is always right—right?" Well, not necessarily. No matter what you try to achieve as a manager, experience dictates that without happy employees you'll never have truly happy customers. And customers often know a lot more about what they want than what they need. So satisfying customers alone, without regard to satisfying employees, and by extension, vendors and other stakeholders, won't guarantee long-term business success.

Then I get the "Wall Street" answer: "The most important purpose of business, for corporations at least, is to make money for its shareholders." Many companies certainly behave exclusively this way, and sooner or later, their weak value proposition for customers and employees gets them into trouble. Stock prices go down, customers defect, and the competition becomes the beneficiary.

Another response is to "create jobs." By now you have probably figured out that this can't be the whole purpose either.

Here's a very socialistic answer: "Corporations exist to efficiently supply goods and services and stimulate community development." Sounds great, but not too many investors will line up behind that philosophy!

The true idealists say, "The reason corporations exist is to steward resources to meet the needs of the world." I actually like that one, but it's tough to measure and even tougher to implement. Perhaps some day the human race will indeed evolve and truly recognize the limitations of natural resources on our planet and we may then reconsider this visionary definition if only because we will no longer have any choice.

Here is a definition I've come up with that seems to meet all of the most reasonable tests:

Corporations exist to **build profitable relationships** with their constituencies: investors, customers, employees, suppliers and the community.

Of course, if you accept this definition, you might then have some difficulty establishing which constituencies are the most important to you. My view is that each constituency is just as important as another and that each is unique in the perception of the value(s) that are exchanged. I suggest then that the key operating word is "profitable," certainly a relative term in the eyes of each beholder. Today we seem to have in fact forgotten that the word "commerce" actually means "to exchange value between parties so that both believe they have profited."

This definition of the fundamental business purpose involves building profitable relationships with their constituencies:

▲ INVESTORS exchange financial capital at risk for returns on their investment in the form of stock appreciation and or dividends.

▲ CUSTOMERS typically exchange cash for products and services that they perceive have equal or greater value than the proffered price.

▲ EMPLOYEES exchange their energy, time, and, increasingly often these days, their intellectual property and even their health for compensation, learning, advancement, and so on.

▲ SUPPLIERS seek to have a preferred status with their clients and endeavor to get a predictable flow of business at a price that allows them to remain competitive.

▲ THE COMMUNITY demands that its laws are honored, taxes are paid, economic development occurs and that the environment is only positively impacted by business decisions. In return, the community provides infrastructure, incentives, and many intangibles to the corporations.

You can see that each constituency has different expectations and perceptions of value being exchanged. Combining these into one definition takes our thinking about the purpose of business far beyond the narrow views noted earlier. This is the real essence of what we do in business—we manage relationships and as a result we create value exchanges.

Historically, corporate governance has been about fealty to shareholders. Yet more and more directors on boards of corporations are realizing that focus on profit alone fails to grow a company's maximum overall worth, ignoring as it does contributions to value available from customer good will and employee motivation.

As an illustration of this, here is an excerpt from a blue-ribbon commission report from the National Association of Corporate Directors (NACD) that clearly shows the trend toward a broader stakeholder view in describing the role of the board:

> Boards of directors bear primary responsibility to the corporation's owners—its shareholders—and should be committed to maximizing shareholder wealth in the long run. To ensure effective representation of all shareholders, boards should have a majority of independent directors.
>
> Experienced directors recognize and accept the fact that the reality of the issues they deal with turns out to be far more complicated than "total and sole responsibility to our shareholders." The value of shareholder returns depends, in no small measure, on several important corporate stake-

holders, including employees, customers, suppliers, and local communities.

An effective board must, therefore, be aware of the legitimate claims stakeholders may have on the corporation, and be prepared to see to it that such claims are equitably honored.

As the Commission suggests, the breadth and depth of our key relationships in all directions equals our collective ability to get the job done.

So if relationship building is so important, why are so many business people focused upon so much else? In the next chapter, The Relationship Advantage, we will explore exactly why such narrow thinking and behavior makes little, if any, business sense and how top-of-the-line relationship management empowers individuals and companies to competitive success.

CHAPTER KEY POINTS

▲ In business, our responses, ultimate impact and feelings of job satisfaction depend entirely upon how we develop and utilize a powerbase of relationships largely of our own making.

▲ Informal relationships, more than ever, provide the professional "glue" and stability that most accurately determines our ability to get results.

▲ Power, quite simply, is one's ability to cause an event to happen or not to happen, that is, to get things done (or not).

▲ Power operates inside organizations by flowing through informal human networks and grapevines in which true cooperation is not formalized.

▲ Corporations exist to build profitable relationships with their constituencies: investors, customers, employees, suppliers and the community.

CHAPTER 2

THE RELATIONSHIP ADVANTAGE

"If I have seen further,
it is by standing on the
shoulders of giants."

—Sir Isaac Newton, 1675

Quick! Can you name the two biggest risks in business today? The global economy and aggressive competition, you say? Changing population demographics and consumer levels of education? Do I hear: The World Wide Web and rapid technological change?

While all these are certainly daunting factors, I can't place any of them at the top of my list. To my mind, the most risky propositions today are *loss of customer focus* and *slow execution*. It is these two factors, I believe, that will be responsible for doing most companies in over the course of the next decade, hands down.

More than ever before in history, capital and products appear to be far less important for developing a sustainable competitive advantage than cultivating loyal customers and employees. I'm certain that time to market, time to decisions, and time to partner-like relationships will determine most of tomorrow's winners and losers. For that reason, any company with a high-performance, customer-focused organization is a CEO's dream.

Products and technologies change quickly as communications and information technology shorten the time frame for competitors to learn and imitate in every field. The real battle has now become the tooth-and-nails competition for quality relationships. Though a tough one to emulate, exceptional relationship quality throughout the value chain of a business is worth fostering because it attracts and retains both customers and employees even in the face of breakdowns, reversals, and slow growth. That's the meaning of the title of this chapter, The Relationship Advantage.

Achieving such advantage requires a customer-focused strategy driven by customer-focused teams, trained in a customer-focused culture and operating as a high-powered, customer-focused sales, marketing development, and delivery system. Experience shows that two of these—the strategy and the system—may be the easiest to come by since many companies have recently adopted "customer-intimate" strategies complete with customer information databases as supportive tools. Few, however, get the teaming/cultural piece right.

Fred Wiersema, in his book *Customer Intimacy*, defines the concept of his book's title as "a dedication to customer results" organization-wide. Total customer-intimate procedures must emanate from an established set of core values identified by an organization's leadership and carrying a full commitment from upper management to a change-management process that includes significant training and development. Organizations rich in the PowerSkills detailed in this book will be able to fulfill this vision of a high-performance customer focus effectively.

DEAL VERSUS RELATIONSHIP CULTURES

Networking hardware giant Cisco Systems stands out as a strong example of what I mean. Now the dominant player in an industry in which it was once a struggling, small player, Cisco has achieved its leader status on the strength of a finely tuned trinity of customer-focused strategy, systems, and culture.

Despite intense competition in earlier days from 3Com and Cabletron, two scrappers with very similar products in the early nineties, Cisco's founders had believed deeply in the importance of customer focus, establishing a customer-advocacy department on Day One. They went on from there to construct and grow a sturdy customer-focused culture that has succeeded in growing both internally as well as through acquisitions.

But while Cisco was busy formulating high-level executive relationships with large customers and reaching its markets through other customer-based channels, competitor 3Com was becoming "channel-centric," focusing increasingly on lower-end products. Meanwhile Cisco's other competitor, Cabletron, developed another reputation—a company with a rough, take-no-prisoners direct sales division that didn't mind outright strong-arming or upsetting its own customers if such tactics would win a sale. Cabletron struggled to develop other distribution channels but with mixed success.

The employee relations practices of the three companies offered perhaps telling information as well. As Cisco invested heavily in workforce training and development, 3Com recruited hard from the competition with minimal training while Cabletron became notorious for treating its people as expendable resources to be chewed up and spit away. Three companies that began at essentially the same time with similar technology in an emerging market each ended up with very different results. By the end of the nineties, Cisco had become a 12-plus billion-dollar company with a market cap of over 210 billion. By comparison, 3Com's revenues were at 5.4 billion with only a market cap 8.6 billion, and Cabletron was struggling at 1.4 billion in sales with lots of red ink. Cisco won the relationship-advantage prize, no contest, with its customer-focused culture.

Cisco Systems

How does Cisco Systems do it? The new old-fashioned way, of course!

In 1999, Cisco Systems continued to solidify its positioning as "the company for the new economy," in the words of its CEO John Chambers. In simple terms, many companies who need to go "dot-com" view Cisco Systems as synonymous with the Internet! When an MIS manager purchases a router or other Web device from Cisco, it's said, he/she never worries about getting reprimanded or fired for doing so.

How has Cisco achieved its top-of-market branding and how does it stay on top of top of a very battle-prone heap? Is it through superior product technology, high-tech innovation, or technical expertise?

While all those may help, that's not the way Cisco gets the selling job done. Instead, as reported by Lee Grove in the *Wall Street*

Journal in August 1999, Cisco relies primarily on old-fashioned sales methods, PowerSkills thinking and dedicated relationship management!

Its massive sales force, for example, plays down technology, emphasizing "business solutions." And as a result it's not unknown for the president of a major customer firm to remark that he doesn't even understand, from a technical point of view, what he's buying from Cisco. To which a Cisco sales rep is likely to snap, affably: "It actually doesn't matter if you know any of that. What matters is you know that our products are the best!"

Likewise, when a company's buyer expresses doubts about the value of buying from Cisco, comparing product specs with 3Com perhaps, the sales rep might reply: "I'll tell you what you're getting with us: a direct link with the company that's waking up the Internet."

How does this sit with clients and prospective clients? Grove reports in his *Journal* piece that it sits very well. That's because, unlike 3Com and others, Cisco sends a 6,000-rep sales force out to the corporate hinterlands every day of every week to hunt, build, and nurture all its business face-to-face. He quotes one Cisco sales rep commenting that the company has set a formidable bar against its competition.

"They are forced to play a technology game," remarked Carlos Dominguez, top sales executive for Cisco's Northeast sector. Grove adds: "He means that his rivals must pitch the fine points of their products, while Cisco can build on its customer relationships."

"It's a beautiful thing," Mr. Dominguez concludes with a smile.

You bet it is: this time he's speaking about PowerSkills and Cisco's relationship advantage.

RELATIONSHIPS: RESOURCES OR ASSETS?

In the Amazon rainforest you can find slash-and-burn-logging operations going on every day all day long as developers erase literally hundreds of plant and insect species in the blink of an eye. At first glance this all looks like such innocent, civilized "progress," but scientists theorize that in too many cases a significant percent of these lost-forever species had not yet been discovered.

Although many people around the world view this region as a treasure, one that is vital for our survival as a species, others mark the rainforest for a quick buck, more than willing to chop down all its resources and sell off whatever markets will bear. That done, they move along to new acreage, leaving the land they've just despoiled unusable for decades, or longer.

Yet in more urban and so-called sophisticated arenas, many of us go about our business affairs much the same way. There, good business is measured by how many "deals" one can pull off, with the actual people involved viewed as resources or raw materials to use up and discard. Customers, employees, vendors, business partners—all represent momentary fodder to help us "score," "close a deal," or "make a killing," then move on, deal to deal to deal. Should human beings along the way lose out, get fired, go out of business, then, well, so be it, the thinking goes. After all, a deal's a deal, and winners, to paraphrase a saying in eighties-speak, were those that went home with the most toys.

In the case of the rainforest, since we've now looked at the evidence, such slash-and-burn attitudes leave us all with fewer and fewer non-renewable natural resources, a result that will eventually cause environmental mayhem. That's why the truly wise among us can explain why playing the resource game is a sport for fools. In the final analysis, they know, it cannot be won.

It would be much smarter to view business as opportunities, at the same time considering people as assets, similar to resources, yes, but the kind one draws upon and borrows from time to time, not the kind intended for depletion. It was true, for example, many years ago that hikers in a wooded area, large or small, would think nothing of tossing down food wrappers or cigarette butts on a mountain trail as if the natural environment were one big giant trash can. Who cares? went the thinking, let someone else worry about it. But it's a rarity now to come across an outdoor enthusiast who thinks this way. Such anachronistic attitudes stick out like a sore thumb today, viewed by others as callous, hostile, or plain ignorant.

Yet in the business world the notion survives of "use-em-up-and-throw-em-away," in this case meaning people just as frequently as raw materials, equipment, real estate, and other inanimate things. Work and business, seen as a battleground, are not commonly respected as environments to be protected, nurtured, and preserved.

Fortunately, in many places, and in many minds, this is beginning to change. I've observed more and more professionals who recognize the benefits, and common sense, of infusing "relationships-as-assets" thinking into business affairs. Although product-centered orientations still exist, many companies are now shifting their cultures toward relationships whose positive effect on bottom-lines typically generates great buzz. The annual *Fortune Magazine* lists of top companies in various categories suggest that relationship-centered cultures invariably achieve market leadership, are more profitable, and yield higher dividends. In business, nothing gets everyone's complete attention faster than this result.

Wal-Mart: In the Information Business

One of the classic examples of this can be found in the dual-saga of two of America's twentieth century retail titans, Wal-Mart and K-Mart, an epic battle won hands down until recently, by the company Sam Walton built.

The contest began on the eve of the twentieth century, 1899, in Detroit, where K-Mart was born as a modest, newfangled department store known as S.S. Kresge. In those days there had never been anything like Kresge's, a sparkling huge open showroom lined with aisles and aisles of brightly colored merchandise in open bins and on shiny display counters, so unlike the drab, brown, dry goods stores that Americans, up till then, had known.

Under the banner "Nothing over Ten Cents," this bright new company expanded steadily over the next decade so that, by 1912, it had opened 85 stores. The company kept on growing and growing, and by the 1950s consistently ranked in the upper echelons of America's largest merchandise retailers.

American demographics reshuffled in the "fabulous fifties," however, and Kresge's decided it was time for a change. Since the end of World War II, America's suburbs had been pushing families out of the biggest cities, so Kresge management calculated the real money was now to be found away from Main Street, their traditional store locations. By 1961, it was ready to make its move, choosing a whole new look and name: K-Mart. Buoyed by ample reserves of capital, the former little five-and-dime, center-of-town storefronts began popping up as shopping "warehouses" in as many of the new malls and retail plazas sprouting on the outer edges of cities.

About the same time, Sam Walton, in Arkansas, came up with a similar idea, but a different one, and in retrospect, a better one.

Walton rightly surmised that, with K-Mart and other copycat discount retailers vying for the same geographical markets (large suburban and urban areas), a buck might be had in the country's increasingly ignored rural areas.

So, as Kresge began letting go its earlier, more homespun customer base, Walton moved in to usurp the old Kresge ideal with a promise of "everyday low prices." Positioning his stores only in sparsely populated locations, taking care not to build any store so close to another that each might cannibalize the other, he set about creating a corporate structure that was destined to dominate the industry by filling a customer void.

How did Walton do it? Basically by adopting a PowerSkill mindset of conceiving every system in his company as a collaborative venture. Wanting to ensure that every Wal-Mart manager could begin each business day with clear competitive advantages, he established such mechanisms as the following:

▲ "Shared" inventory control, involving several stores within a designated regional area. This way each store could keep its inventory costs low, yet provide predictable access to merchandise by everyone. Unlike their area rivals, individual Wal-Marts needn't maintain deep stocks of store items in order to make them quickly available to its customers. Each store could always trade its stock with another store within an hour or two's driving distance and thus work cooperatively to keep every outlet well-stocked.

▲ An up-to-the-minute customer feedback process in the form of centralized buying information from all Wal-Mart stores across the country and from vendor and supplier info. This consumer information was also shared with vendors/

suppliers so that all were educated daily on buying habits. In this way they could work together to keep specific items on hand and develop new products that could be available quickly. In his book, *The Death of Competition,* author James F. Moore calls this mechanism a stunning example of a "business ecosystem" that can't be beat.

As one might imagine, K-Mart soon began to feel the heat of Walton's intensifying human network and attempted to counter Wal-Mart's attack by throwing new merchandise lines of all kinds at its customers and hoping at least some would stick. K-Mart also constructed in-store cafeterias and other ineffective gimmicks, though little of this helped as Wal-Mart continued gliding onward and upward. By the time the nineties rolled around, Wal-Mart was clearly the industry leader while K-Mart and all the others (Bradlees, Target, Ames) lumped together in a shoulder-to-shoulder campaign for second place. Today, the Walton network annually produces twice as much business in only about ten percent more stores compared with K-Mart. More devastating, net income for K-Mart has plunged steadily, now under 3%, since the nineties began while Wal-Mart has held steady at about 4% for the past 30 years.

In *The Death of Competition,* Moore writes: "Wal-Mart perceives itself as an information company. Sitting atop a continually changing framework for co-evolution, it now leads by understanding better than anyone else the operation of that framework and the associated network of organizations and processes. Wal-Mart thrives because it has the best information about meeting customer needs in a variety of markets with a range of stores, fed by a vast network of suppliers and logistics capabilities. Wal-Mart's prime competitive advantage has become information power—the ability to intelligently spawn and manage new elements of its ecosystem, to take advantage of shifting opportunities, and to meet competition wherever it lies."

CORE RELATIONSHIP ASSUMPTIONS

In so many companies, executives talk about the importance of human capital but behave otherwise. The problem lies at the heart of their core assumptions about relationships. Do they really view them as assets or merely resources? Refer to Exhibit 2.1, Core Relationship Assumptions. The left column summarizes those aspects that comprise the view of relationships as resources. The right column describes the contrasting view of relationships as assets.

▶ **EXHIBIT 2.1 Core Relationship Assumptions**

Relationships as RESOURCES	Relationships as ASSETS
Product Centered Planning	Relationship Centered Planning
Focus on Competition	Focus on the Customer
Compete	Collaborate
Use People	Grow People
Only Invest in Tangibles	Attend to Intangibles
Go It Alone	Partnerships
Feature/Benefit/Competitive Deal Culture	**Solution Oriented/Collaborative Relationship Culture**

We can use this framework to compare the core relationship assumptions of K-Mart and Wal-Mart in the mid-nineties, just before a new, customer-centered CEO took K-Mart's reigns in 1995 and begin shifting the discounter more in Wal-Mart's direction. When we look item by item, we note immediately a stark contrast, in light of our discussion of deal vs. relationship cultures. When viewed side by side, Wal-Mart, throughout all the years of its epic battle with K-Mart, just couldn't lose. It was a clear relationship winner on all fronts, consistently creating alliances as assets, not resources, and wielding them to superior competitive advantage.

Exhibit 2.2 is a comparison of these assumptions. Note how K-Mart exemplified the *resources* mindset while Wal-Mart displayed attitudes in the *assets* column.

THE SHIFT IN THINKING TO CUSTOMER INTIMACY

Despite the impressive case of Wal-Mart's ultimate dominance over K-Mart, a testament to relationship-centered planning over product-centered, three decades of mainly product-centered planning in American business have left us with a formidable corporate legacy. Though it has helped us create incredibly complex and powerful organizations over the same period, trust in the workplace and marketplace has largely deteriorated. That same complexity has made too many companies difficult to do business with. Product quality has become, in many instances, superb, but service quality has yet to catch up. In spite of all the talk today about teams and quality engineering, the intensity of the service problem, essentially a relationship one, remains. To the smart eye, of course, this also signals opportunity.

▶ **EXHIBIT 2.2 Comparison of Relationship Assumptions**

Relationships as RESOURCES: K-Mart (until 1995)	Relationships as ASSETS: Wal-Mart (through its history)
Product-centered planning: Lots of merchandise, inventory, and gimmicks.	**Relationship-centered planning:** Web of alliances with other stores & vendors and suppliers considered paramount to understanding customer wishes.
Focus on competition: Strategy of competing with similar rivals in the largest target market areas; customer is told: "We will match any competitors' price".	**Focus on the customer:** Information and feedback systems designed to keep managers informed of customer wishes, philosophy of "everyday low prices" reign.
Use people: Traditional employee pay policies (low wages, no incentives).	**Grow people:** Employee incentive policies, extensive employee training, free-flow of communication.
Invest only in tangibles: Deep stocks of merchandise based on management guesswork not customer feedback, capital equipment, facilities, or acquisitions.	**Attend to intangibles:** Value-driven learning environment for employees, refusal to rigidly commit to specific product lines, displays or departments, i.e., committed to flexibility & change.
Go it alone: Major CEO initiatives focused internally, e.g., cost-control of gross margins, increased accountability from managers, mandate to keep all stores "clean."	**Partnerships:** Everywhere!

How could this decline in service quality happen? Increasing complexity, and especially technology, has meant that the corner-store style of business relationships has gotten replaced with impersonal, intemperate technical interfaces, efficient for simple transactions but all too inappropriate for many other functions. For example, try ordering a small business telephone system or applying for a business loan. A nightmare.

How about clarifying a billing error, getting an insurance claim paid or—heaven forbid—resolving a conflict with a government agency? Expect a week of nightmares!

As consumers, we want low prices, high quality, a large assortment and convenience, to name the most important factors. Though many non-human systems have been created for us with huge benefits unthinkable thirty years ago—ATM machines, intelligent call routing, and buying on the Web come immediately to mind—much has also been created with brand new, never-known-before hassles built in. That's why the pendulum has begun swinging back to relationship building as a differentiator. Only the human touch, when done right, supported by a true relationship culture, can resolve this dilemma.

Recent business books have begun heralding such a swing in thinking, namely improving competitiveness dramatically by paying attention to human assets. We've also begun seeing terms appear like relationship marketing, customer intimacy, customer bonding, collaboration, and loyalty-based management. All represent key concepts that are surely on the right track.

Yet, if this is so, why have these terms gone mainstream, yet fail to fully resonate in the business community? What is needed is a way to assist individuals in concretely visualizing their implementation. *PowerSkills* provides a reality-based focus on raising specific competencies of the needed building blocks. By developing individuals in an organization in such a way that their personal use of relationship-management skills becomes truly effective, businesses can pay attention to human assets and these can finally become visible and widespread.

VALUING RELATIONSHIPS IN BUSINESS

Art reflects culture. That's why business best-seller books reflect the tenor of our times. If we scan best-sellers of the last 25 years, for example, we can notice an interesting contrast between those published at the start of this period and those more prevalent today. Clearly, a shift in thinking has been occurring, and our book titles have reflected it. Take a brief look with me at the titles of best-sellers and you'll see what I mean:

From a Previous Era

1972   *The Art of Getting Your Own Sweet Way*
1975   *Winning through Intimidation*
1978   *Looking Out for Number One*
1982   *The Art of the Deal*

More Recently

1993   *The One to One Marketing Future: Building Relationships
One Customer at a Time*
1995   *Building Strategic Relationships*
1996   *Customer Intimacy*
1996   *The Loyalty Effect*
1999   *Customers.com*

In two decades, book titles have swung from an opportunistic tone to today's louder cry for more relationship-integrated business models. In his 1982 mega-seller *Megatrends,* James Naisbitt accurately predicted this shift: We're now living in a world of "high tech requiring high touch." Naisbitt foresaw this trend as inevitable. Now we really know what he meant.

DRIVERS OF THE CHANGE

It's not hard to imagine how and why this change has come about. Global competitiveness has taken our world by storm over the last twenty years, first creeping up on us, and then gathering thunder throughout the nineties. As a result, people have experienced a loss in human connection. Where once being an employee felt like belonging to a family (the so-called corporate-parent model), now employee status conveys a warning: "Beware! Tomorrow could very well be your last day. Prepare yourself for it now! Oh, and get back to work, and work *harder!*"

Consider the following: outsourcing, re-engineering, rapid product cycles, information networks, the trend toward virtual organizations, the pace of acquisitions, joint ventures, and partnering. Combine all these and you've got one very unsettling employment landscape. This leaves us with a quite formidable relationship management challenge—the need to cultivate respect for individual employees while not promising them that anything will last.

This suggests a customer relationship management challenge as well: demonstrating that we as companies truly care about our customers, despite contemporary seller-buyer gulfs due to massive, complicated organization.

STEPS TO CLIENT LOYALTY

In the early eighties, the transition period from the Look-Out-for-Number-One business philosophy of the seventies to the attempts at customer intimacy in our present world, an article in *Harvard*

Business Review (September/October 1983) caught many readers' eyes. Called *After the Sale Is Over…* by Ted Levitt, it coined a term which would usher in a new business paradigm: "relationship management." This represented a new field of inquiry that was, Levitt wrote, probably "worth studying."

This "special field all its own" (relationship management), the article continued, "…is as important to preserving and enhancing the intangible asset commonly known as 'goodwill' as is the management of hard assets. The fact that it is probably more difficult makes hard work at it that much more important."

Before this article, not much had been written about business relationships in quite this way. For the first time, Levitt likened them to hard assets in terms of their importance so that, soon after the article's appearance, it seemed the dam broke loose on the whole matter. Many business analysts and authors began studying the subject, and in 1991 author, consultant, and investor Regis McKenna broke out of the pack with what would become a seminal work in the area, *Relationship Marketing*. The race was now on to understand and attempt to successfully implement relationship strategies that, as McKenna explained, meant business had evolved from "tricking" and/or "blaming" the customer to "investing" in the customer. How right he was.

Traditionally, product companies use the term "customers," and professional service firms (i.e., accounting, consulting, law) refer to their "clients" as a more intimate description. We all have internal and external "clients" today for our goods, services, and ideas. Increasingly the term "customer" is being dropped as more intimate relationships form, as you will see in Exhibit 2.3, Steps to Client Loyalty.

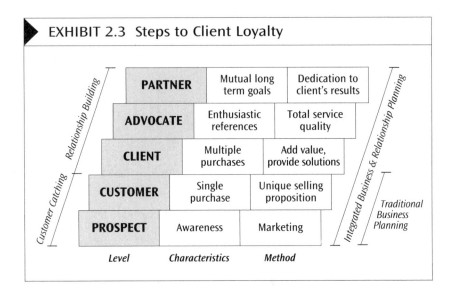

EXHIBIT 2.3 Steps to Client Loyalty

Level	Characteristics	Method
PARTNER	Mutual long term goals	Dedication to client's results
ADVOCATE	Enthusiastic references	Total service quality
CLIENT	Multiple purchases	Add value, provide solutions
CUSTOMER	Single purchase	Unique selling proposition
PROSPECT	Awareness	Marketing

In this illustration we can track the stages by which the so-called customer-investment concept naturally evolves. At the lowest level we observe how strongly deal-making holds sway. Here potential customers are often seen as *prospects,* to be "gotten," "won over," or "made a deal with."

Once such a deal is made, your prospect becomes a real *customer,* with you having absorbed a significant acquisition cost. Despite the investment, individuals are still not seen in a relationship light until the next level, *client.* This term is defined as a customer who buys frequently, at least two times or more. At this point we are beginning to emphasize relationship building.

It's here too where, if we are relationship-wise, we begin investing in our clients—keeping them advised of new products and services, surveying their opinions of our service, offering special discounts, value-added features, or just plain giving products or services away. Example: A telecommunications company might throw in an extra dozen cell phones to a client company who places a huge order. "Don't worry about it," says the sales executive. "I want you to have them." You're becoming friends.

At the next level, our relationships become stronger than ever. Here clients become outright *advocates,* literally working for us now, referring new prospects and customers our way, and supporting us through word of mouth. Having experienced total service quality from us, they are confident in our problem resolution and ability to anticipate their needs. They'll even offer us good ideas and feedback with little prodding.

The top level is reserved for *partner,* representing the most client intimate relationship we could possibly enjoy. At this level, long-term customers are ours to lose, and if we are truly relationship-smart, we will use our PowerSkills to see to it that such investment somehow takes place at every step along the way. As partners we plan our futures together.

Consider this: Can you offer some special knowledge or extra assistance to a prospect, for example—a bit of mentoring or some other "industry intelligence"? Perhaps you can you give away a lesser version of your product to a prospect or allow a prospect to use it for a short time, to solve a real problem? If so, your relationship would begin before any money changes hands. You would also be showing your prospect how effective your product or service is. An investment, then, in your prospect could dramatically accelerate your sales success.

If you divided up your world into prospects, customers, clients, advocates, and partners, who would you put in each category? Is your organization achieving the higher levels of relationships?

ENTROPY: DON'T LET YOUR
CLIENTS GET LOST IN THE SHUFFLE!

In business, entropy is always the wolf outside our door. The dictionary defines "entropy" as "the tendency toward uniform inertness" and "a measure of unavailability of energy for work in a natural process." Unfortunately, we are always in danger of falling into this state, slowly becoming unavailable to our clients as we get sidetracked by other clients or go all-out to sign up new ones. Entropy meanwhile sits quietly on the front porch, unraveling bonds we thought we had so carefully wrapped together. We get busy on new customers' needs and we automatically move away from older, established ones. One day we wake up and the older ones have left us for someone else.

The ebb and flow of our relationships is all about intimacy and separation, the approach/avoidance syndrome. That's why maintaining client relationships requires real effort beyond merely providing good products and services. It's all too easy to do good work for a small group of clients while ignoring many others you've come to take for granted, assuming they will always be there. We always figure we will get back in touch with the others eventually, when we have more time. Yet often such idle times never come and the result is that our solid, long-time clients get lost in the shuffle.

You, of course, want to avoid this syndrome. One proven role model you might learn from is a company that has refused for decades to ever take its clients for granted, going on 80 years now. It's a superb example of how to ensure steady and stable relationship management.

This company is called Snap-On Tools and you've seen their trucks rumbling past you now and then on a highway or taking a hard turn into a gas station or industrial park, but you've probably never paid much attention. Yet since the day Snap-On opened its doors, it has been sending its ever-enlarging fleet of trucks out over America's roads and byways to visit with mechanics of all types and to let them see and touch their wares. The company has never deviated from one amazing and simple idea: selling high-quality tools to those who need them—auto, truck, and airplane mechanics—by literally driving the tools out to their customers' workplaces, setting them down in front of their customers' eyes, and placing them directly in their hands.

Even today, as hardware and auto parts stores expect their customers to come to them, Snap-On assumes otherwise, refusing to open stores and staying true to the good, swift, to-the-point-of-purchase service that has allowed them to maintain market leadership for generations. In 1999, still in the lead in its industry, Snap-On's 1.7 billion-dollar sales volume includes earnings of $150 million and a 60% share of this three-billion-dollar automotive-tool market. Its willingness to deliver its sales force, i.e., drivers, as well as its products directly to its 1.25 million customers has earned it the most loyal of followings.

"It looks archaic," admits Snap-On chairman and CEO Robert A. Cornog in the book *Radical Marketing* (Harper-Collins, 1999) by Sam Hill and Glenn Rifkin, "but instead of real estate on the corner with the fixed costs of people, taxes, and overhead, we have a very powerful business out there at the point of sale."

Rather than spend huge volumes on advertising, Snap-On instead clearly invests in its customer/partners. In 1994, it funded a two million-dollar dedication to auto mechanics using print ads that asked, "When did you first learn the value of a good mechanic?"

Today, framed copies of these ads, report Hill and Rifkin, still adorn hundreds of auto shops around the country, whether serviced or not by Snap-On Tools.

Beyond the smart marketing approach, how does Snap-On do it? CEO Cornog's response is so simple, so unassuming, yet so exactly on target: "We understand people who make a living with our products, with tools," he says. In an industry that has generally taken its customer base for granted since the very beginnings, Snap-On clearly stands out as a fine example of a company with a better way.

Now this question: Do you understand your customers as well? Are your employees so devoted they too would jump out of bed early each morning and climb into a truck loaded with thousands of your company's gadgets, then drive hundreds of miles a day in a mission to make customer contact? Snap-On Tools meets with each one of its customers face to face by the end of every week—how many of your customers do *you* see?

If you don't feel satisfied with your answer, maybe you need to get clearer about what a productive client relationship truly is. What are the essential components of relationships that deliver value? What makes such value continue? How can you incorporate such value components to ensure you retain and grow your own relationship advantage?

In the next chapter, we'll examine relationship components by viewing them in the context of a relationship equation. We'll also explore implications for each and learn the specific benefits derived by companies who have mastered and maintained them. We'll then be ready to move on to the secret weapons that ensure these components remain in view—the five PowerSkills.

CHAPTER KEY POINTS

▲ More than ever, capital and products appear to be far less important for developing a sustainable competitive advantage than cultivating loyal customers and employees.

▲ Achieving competitive advantage requires a customer-focused strategy like no other, one driven by customer-focused teams trained in a customer-focused culture.

▲ The pendulum has begun swinging back to relationship building as a differentiator.

▲ We can improve our competitiveness dramatically by paying attention to human assets.

▲ Those who are relationship-smart invest in their clients.

▲ Maintaining great customer relationships requires real effort beyond merely providing good products and services.

CHAPTER 3

THE RELATIONSHIP EQUATION

"The whole of science is nothing more than a refinement of everyday thinking."

—Albert Einstein

A few days after returning from a pleasant mid-winter Florida vacation, I was driving down the potholed beltway that curves around Boston, Route 128, also euphemistically known as "America's Technology Highway," when I hit an icy patch in the cruising lane. Snow and ice on the road is not, of course, a welcome sight when you've just spent a glorious, sunny golf and fishing vacation week in Palm Beach, but there I was, skidding over the ice, successfully recovering, breathing a sigh of relief, until suddenly—blam!—a truck behind me went out of control on the same ice and rammed into me. Fortunately, not too much damage occurred to either of our vehicles or us.

While filling out my accident report the next day, I placed a call to my business and personal insurance agency of twelve years to ask a few questions. Unfortunately for me, my agency had been sold to a larger company three months earlier and the woman who answered the phone that day not only did not know me but also brusquely informed me she couldn't help me. "You have to call a different office, we don't handle that here," she snapped, adding, "We have a new system." So I got off the phone and dialed a new number to ask my questions.

When I called this different office, another representative answered, also somewhat impatient with me. She explained what she could about the matters I wanted to discuss but when I asked her if I would have loss-of-use coverage since the accident was not my fault, she was less helpful. "Am I covered for a rental vehicle while my car is in the shop?" I asked.

Once again I was told I would have to call someplace else, this time the insurance company of the other driver to get a clearance for that. Plainly, it was all up to me, notions of "service-America" notwithstanding. I was a completely unrecognized number in dealing with these two offices.

Not only was no one willing to go even slightly out of their way to help me, no one had even asked, and I'm sure hadn't really cared, if I was physically okay as a result of the accident, i.e., had I been hurt? Though I am not one who needs any special sympathy from strangers, I nonetheless found the whole episode more interesting from a customer value standpoint.

Later that day I set off to see Billy Pascucci, owner of Cape Ann Auto Body, who has mended my family's cars for years. Though usually my wife, Judi, made such arrangements, this time I chose to drop over and make the appointment myself. Needless to say, especially after my insurance phone calls, I was not looking forward one bit to what I might find there. In such frame of mind, I was about to be shocked.

Driving my now-battered Audi into Billy's lot, tall and lanky Billy Pascucci himself came striding out, looking for all the world like a modern-day Abe Lincoln, wagging those Honest-Abe whiskers on his chin. "Hey, Jim, say, what can I do for you today?" he chirped, looking over my bashed-in fender. "Looks like you had a little run-in." I started to reply but he quickly added, "Well, are you okay? Anybody hurt? Y'know, I can fix cars real good but I can't fix up people. I hope you're all right."

I said I was. He acted genuinely relieved to hear this and, even though I hadn't made an appointment, he invited me to relax in his waiting room while he finished up with another customer. "I'll get right to you after that," he said. As I sat there, I observed his professional and down-to-earth style with his other customers, noting how he quickly came up with solutions for each situation amiably, responsively, attentively. I also watched him juggle time and attention with two insurance adjusters who popped in unexpectedly, as did other regular customers here and there.

I also noticed hundreds of endorsement cards on the wall from past customers who raved about the service Billy had provided them. No wonder the buzz up and down Boston's North Shore labeled his the best body shop around. In fact, when you got your car from Billy, it was (at no extra charge) washed and polished in his detailing area. He always let you know when to expect the car, how much it would cost and he always came in within his estimate. Billy had established a successful business upon a foundation I call the Relationship Equation.

RELATIONSHIPS—THE ESSENTIAL EQUATION

The biggest myth going is the one that says relationships are all about "clicking" or are the result of some vague form of chemistry or due to just plain luck. Yes, while it's true that personality and chemistry and luck of the draw do play a part in relationship building, they're rarely the whole of it. Relationships can be constructed, grown, fashioned, championed, fabricated, turned around, re-built, reborn, and materialized. Just consider my dealings with Billy. His style of customer interaction made my relationship with him inevitable. Why would I take my car to anyone else?

Relationships can and do appear out of thin air but they don't have to start that way. In fact they usually do not. Instead, good relationships are complex combinations of essential qualities, without which they cannot exist. We are always capable of initiating and maintaining a relationship as long as we remember what must go into it.

What's the easiest and surest way to do this? Consider the *Relationship Equation:*

Relationships = Trust + Value + Dialogue

$$R = T + V + D$$

All relationships in your business or personal life can be described by this equation. It says that the quality of a *relationship* is made up of the quality of the components of *trust, value* and *dialogue* (on-going interaction). Remove any one of these and the relationship will deteriorate—any two out of the three is simply not good enough.

Take, for example, a relationship with a professional financial planner who advises you on your estate plan, asset allocation, manages your portfolio, and prepares your tax returns. Trust must be absolute for this relationship to work. Value must be demonstrated in the form of business and financial counsel that helps you make better decisions and increase your wealth. Frequent and easy-to-understand reports, planning sessions, communication, and alerts throughout the year achieve an ongoing dialogue that reinforces the trust and value in the relationship.

As we noted earlier, many American companies have all but ignored this equation as organizational complexity has increased the distance between sellers and buyers. The fast boil of global competitiveness and the urgency to pile on more and more technology "enhancements" have not helped the situation. Somewhere along the way, the human touch got lost

IBM—The Road Back

At the time of my initial visit to its Armonk, New York Headquarters in October 1992, the Board of IBM had, for the first time in its history, "fired" its CEO. The company had also just begun to use several retained executive search firms to identify a replacement and was embarking on other searches to fill other key posts. Although it was an established business practice for other companies to bring in consultants to search for top talent, IBM had previously preferred to "grow their own" from within.

The parking lot outside the main doors was unexpectedly empty. I stepped inside to greet one of the company's program managers in Executive Resources, Richard Achilles. It was his new job to design and lead the search process for a number of executive slots and to work directly with the search firms. My particular assignment was to help IBM find and select a VP of Marketing.

There had been a reduction in the headquarters staff, and the building seemed eerily quiet to me even though Achilles assured me that the building was generally a sedate place. Escorting me around to various executive offices, Achilles delicately briefed me on why IBM badly needed my firm's help to find a VP of Marketing. In the most open and professional way he could, Achilles revealed the wrenching change IBM was going through. I could tell that this once-mighty giant was in the throws of a significant, and heretofore unparalleled, renewal process. It would be difficult to attract executives from high-flying companies that had the right stuff to be part of the rejuvenation.

Sometime later Lou Gerstner was selected as CEO and within months this new leader from R.J. Reynolds had asserted himself as the person to re-energize the firm and give it organizational focus. Even though the company's troubles were far from over, Gerstner nonetheless soon won the confidence of the community of executives and leaders in this tightly woven culture.

Although everyone knew that it was time to put new coping mechanisms in place, few had been comfortable with the idea of any outsider coming in and totally revamping the organization and culture. Gerstner even replaced the three-core-values statement adopted by the late T.J. Watson with his own eight-values statement. Gerstner also shocked a lot of people, IBM insiders and out, when he insisted, "The last thing that IBM needs now is a new strategy." And the trade press and industry analysts slammed Gerstner immediately for not putting forth a fresh vision.

Many questioned that a tobacco executive could lead a computer systems company anyway. He was not a high-tech guy; but, as he said at the time, he was a computer consumer and he knew the company needed to rekindle a primary concentration on its consumers and to listen to them hard. Here was a legendary company ripping with technology and badly needing to get great products to market. But, more importantly, here was a wounded family needing to align all its members to the many great goals that had been previously well managed and consistently executed to fantastic results. For me, Gerstner was saying IBM needed to rekindle its relationship advantage, the very heart and soul that had elevated this high-tech pioneer to pre-eminence in years gone by.

Gerstner knew the company had lost its way sometime in the 1980s. It had stopped listening to its customers, effectively ending its dialogue with customers and, as a result, debilitating or destroying its essential relationships. One top company technical executive even went so far as to refer, disdainfully, to IBM's traditionally well-regarded, respected direct sales force as "a bunch of blue-suited relationship managers without content." Well, maybe, I thought, when I heard that remark, but it was those same "relationship managers" who had built an exceptional company, one that Gerstner was apparently determined to bring back and make great again.

A corollary to the Relationship Equation might read like this: Continuity begets consistency, which begets trust, instilling confidence both inside and outside an organization. Lou Gerstner had the right idea.

A MOVEMENT PICKS UP STEAM

One company that has led the charge to return the relationship equation to day-to-day business is the much-heralded Internet trailblazer business Amazon.com. By now everyone knows about this remarkable on-line merchant that began as a bookseller that makes available millions of books, CDs, DVDs, videos, and goods by auction and quickly delivers them to your door in at most a couple of days.

Although I've never spoken with anyone there directly, I have a relationship with Amazon.com. I can easily and quickly access their product anytime of the day or night, seven days a week, and each book I order always comes with a substantial discount. Just as important, the "people" at Amazon.com keep up a dialogue with me, notifying me on a regular basis of new releases from authors I'm interested in or of books on subject areas I might tend to buy.

They also provide book reviews to help me with my selection and will even allow me to review a book and publish that review on-line, right beside the advertisement for the book itself. Once you purchase your first book there, you are connected to their system in a consistent way via a two-way dialogue in pursuit of products that carry high value. What better new world illustration could one find for $R = T + V + D$?

Others are finding their own way to the Relationship Equation. We can now see organizations like Amazon's chief competitor Barnesandnoble.com using a "clicks and mortar" (web and physical stores) approach to close the gap with Amazon's outstanding user-friendliness. The truth is that only a concerted effort to incorporate relationship-skills thinking into an organization-wide relationship culture will succeed.

THE HIDDEN VALUE OF BUSINESS

Once a positive Relationship Equation has been firmly set in place, great benefits await all parties involved. Commitment from customers and employees runs high as long-term, trusting, win-win alliances replace more traditional seller-buyer and employer-employee divisions. There are bonuses to this style of commerce as well, "hidden values" gained by your business.

For one thing, close relationships with your customers can save you money. You won't have to do nearly as much advertising or hard selling or promotion. Often simply talking about a potential new project, in the midst of a conversation about other things, will win you business. Continued income, then, develops naturally.

The same will be true for your strong relationships with suppliers. Often, these would also be willing to upgrade you to a higher-quality product, or provide the extra service. It's a confirmation that, in the end, business relationship skills will yield success more reliably than will technical skills.

Have you ever called a plumber or painter to come over to your house chiefly because you'd gotten to know him, even though you realize he might be not quite as good as one of his competitors? Your developed relationship with him makes it hard for you to "desert" him and be disloyal. All this goes to show that the most important selling work in a company, when all is said and done, will be the result of human networks.

In fact, satisfaction from stakeholders can attain such levels that even when the product or service temporarily slips to second place, or when some formidable competition suddenly appears on the scene, boasting of dramatic improvements, steadfast loyalty keeps customers on board, refusing to desert the ship. In such instances, widespread knowledge of the marginal or temporary inferiority of the product becomes irrelevant as business for the company stays level or even grows larger, deepening, in some cases, the company's market share.

A real-life example of this would be a perennially struggling major league baseball organization like the the Chicago Cubs or the Boston Red Sox. In both cases, outfits that put out their "product" year after year never quite fulfill an implied promise (that their teams are capable of winning a pennant and perhaps even a World Series). Yet their customers (fans), keep paying higher prices for season tickets no matter what, despite annual spring/summer/fall grumbling. Such die-hard baseball consumers never cease to consider their money well-spent.

The Red Sox might be the most illustrative case of all. Cursed, some say, by the sale of Babe Ruth to the New York Yankees back in 1919, the Sox (or "Red Flops" as they frequently are referred to by disappointed-yet-again fans in New England) have not won a World Series since 1918. Although they have made it to Series play now and then, something always mysteriously happens to upset their momentum and allows them to lose it all, in the end.

In 1986, for example, playing against the New York Mets, the Sox were one out away from winning what would have been the final game of the series when a routine ground ball was tapped toward Sox first baseman Bill Buckner. A relatively competent fielder, Buckner somehow, astonishingly, permitted this weak grounder to roll between his legs and over his fielder's glove. The batter reached first base, a Met run scored, and the rest of the series joined the annals of Red Sox infamy. The Mets ultimately won the Series, and the Sox, as people prefer to say every year in Boston, had blown it again.

Yet do Red Sox fans desert the team in droves, take their business to a minor league team, for example (there are two in the area), or watch some other team (like the dreaded Yankees!) on TV? Not on your life! Each year, long before Opening Day in April, Red Sox tickets of all kinds are completely sold out and only scattered grandstand seats are still available for purchase along with a block of seats in the bleachers, which is traditionally for sale only on the day of each game. Fans from Boston even arrange vacations to Florida in February just to watch the Sox at their spring training camp. For whatever mysterious reason, the relationship these consumers have with the Red Sox organization transcends their satisfaction (or lack of it!) with the actual "product."

MASTERING THE POWERSKILLS
OF RELATIONSHIP MANAGEMENT

As we move closer to our examination of the five PowerSkills themselves in the next section of this book, we should first note that, while PowerSkills by themselves may not be sufficient for great success in today's business world, they are the solid differentiator. Combined with the right strategy and values, however, PowerSkills make all the difference. Using the analogy of a physical fitness program, let me show you what I mean.

When we decide to get our bodies in shape, we rarely do so with a life-and-death urgency. Sometimes life is at stake, it's true especially after a heart problem is detected or when someone who is overweight is at great risk because of heightened cholesterol levels.

But most of us decide to join a gym because we believe it would be a good thing for us to do, not because we absolutely have to. Perhaps we want to take a few pounds off, maybe we want to feel a little better, or get some muscle tone before heading out in the summer for the beach. Whatever our reasons, they are typically important but not urgent.

Yet as we begin to work out, at first we take baby steps, walking on the treadmill for ten or fifteen minutes, lifting easy ten- or twelve-pound barbells, stretching slowly and carefully. Only as we begin to push to new levels do we start getting notions in our heads of greater things: running in a road race, for example, maybe even a marathon; lifting heavier weights and setting a lofty goal; learning Yoga so that our stretching becomes as healthfully beneficial as it possibly can. Essentially, what we are engaged in here is working toward mastery, on some level. We are no longer merely "working out"—now we have become focused on attaining a higher plateau.

Effectively incorporating PowerSkills in your professional life tends to move you in the same direction. After observing real results from their implementation, including experiencing a kind of "endorphin high," you will on some level wish to attempt mastery, i.e., to want to push your PowerSkills practice to its limits and see what super results you can achieve through effective collaborations. At that point, utilizing your PowerSkills will be akin to feeling a need to go to the gym after a layoff or vacation. You begin having trouble imagining your work life without them. You draw from them effortlessly, freely, immediately, automatically.

Before long, the practice of PowerSkills becomes a way of life. You are "in flow" with them constantly, not even thinking about how or why you use them, you just do, and that's the end of it. Have you ever imagined you could make a fifteen-minute phone call and accomplish ten or more objectives within such a short time? Consider the following possible results of such a phone chat:

▲ You end up saving a client or colleague you are speaking with a hefty sum of money.

▲ You inform your client of a recent trend.

▲ Your client or colleague offers you an introduction to an important connection.

▲ You both brainstorm a few helpful ideas that get a new project approved.

▲ You inform your client of two major players in their industry.

▲ You offer some requested advice.

▲ You are told about a new technology that will help you immensely.

▲ You provide some added visibility for your client by planning to include her in one of your promotional efforts.

▲ Your client or colleague invites you to a desirable business or cultural event.

▲ You leave your client/colleague feeling uplifted, encouraged, much more positive than when you first began to chat.

Could five or more of these value exchanges occur in one fifteen-minute call? Sounds unlikely, does it not? Well, if you haven't yet incorporated PowerSkills into your day-to-day work life, it probably is. But I can assure you, once you learn to get into the relationship-management flow, this level is quite possible to achieve, indeed. The best people I know collaborate like this all the time.

A PERSONAL AND COMPANY DISCIPLINE

Remember my story about those insurance administrators who kept flipping me over to some other department or phone number? None of them seemed to care a hoot about my particular problems, and not one bothered to ask if I had been hurt in my accident (as Billy did, first thing). All sounded self-important, busy, impatient, robotic.

Whenever we encounter such insensitive corporate "ambassadors" (could be a rude waiter, overbearing sales rep, boorish manager), it's easy and natural to blame the individual first, their company second. This employer, of course, loses our future business right on the spot, but when we get right down to it, we actually personalize the incident, labeling the individual non-caring and insensitive, assuming the buck really starts and stops with the person.

But when you think about it, it's really not so. The truth is that poor professional behavior usually derives from poor training, a deal-oriented culture or perhaps a demoralized one. If we wish to be accurate, we actually may want to inspect the organization, not just the company rep (who's just doing what he or she would be doing under anyone else's employ). It's the company's lack of commitment to ensuring that its people treat the rest of us well that sticks out when compared to organizations who take the trouble to get it right. Those insurance reps who shuffled me around were never trained to handle my call any other way. They simply moved this disembodied voice on the phone along and went on to concentrate on other matters.

At least a few organizations would've handled me very differently, that is, with care. When we experience this, it knocks our socks off, we're that shocked! Home Depot, for example, never fails to make me feel at home with its helpful, orange-aproned associates who wander about each store, sidling up to folks like me who linger in an aisle looking confused. "Is there something I can help you find, sir?" they ask with a warm smile and walk you right to the part of the store you are interested in. Now that's relationship management I can identify with!

The famous Ritz-Carlton is another case in point, especially the one in Boston. Neatly uniformed hotel staff seem to actually enjoy assisting residents and patrons in need, whatever the problem on their minds. In fact, personnel at the Ritz, from the "bottom" on up, are actually empowered to solve a customer's problem right there on the spot, even if it costs the hotel a few dollars. Specifically, any solution to a customer's problem can be set in motion by anyone on the hotel's staff, up to a spending limit of $1800, not only by a manager but by concierge staff, desk clerks, bell men, door men, and elevator operators. Each such employee is authorized to spend money on a customer if it will help.

Their final remark, upon servicing a customer, is the best part for me. When requested to help with even a problem as minor as transferring your phone call to a room or department, Ritz personnel have been trained to respond, "It would be my pleasure." Small wonder the Ritz remains, after so many decades, at the top of America's most revered hotels list. Their kind of tradition deserves to continue.

To achieve true relationship advantage, relationship-savvy business leaders recognize that, although they may understand PowerSkills personally, and perhaps always exercised them innately, they absolutely must find ways to transfer these same skills to others. The real work of an organization will always get done through relationship networks. Simply recognizing the value of such interconnectedness arms a leader with powerful ideas and actions to take because most competitors, by contrast, continue to depend on only a few key relationships and leave it at that. In doing so, they lose out on the benefits that even small increases in the breadth, depth, and quality of their important relationships will create.

Since relationships strengthen or deteriorate all the time, entropy, remember, is always chipping away at the edges. As a result, all too often our most productive relationships get short shrift as we begin paying less and less attention to them. Effective professionalism, however, *requires* our continued follow-up and maintenance and this can't be done without training our people to carry out relationship skills every day. Those who keep these skills in the forefront will be among those who excel, as the Home Depot, the Ritz and other customer-relationship masters have shown.

PROXIMITY BEATS SIMILARITY

People tend to associate with those similar to themselves. This is known as the similarity principle as exemplified by the old cliché "birds of a feather, flock together." When people meet in cyberspace, they typically come together based on similar attitudes, skillsets, interests, but this clustering can limit their interactions. Yet another principle of relationship mastery is the proximity principle, that is, "proximity beats similarity." By this we mean, that physical proximity and frequency of interaction encourages cooperation and expands relationship possibilities. As Diana Eck of the Harvard Pluralism Project puts it, "Stereotypes vanish quickly after people meet face-to-face."

When we develop relationships with people whom we do things with, not necessarily with people already conspicuously similar to ourselves, the creative tensions between us and the resulting fusion of our dissimilar ideas create a new common bond. With it, new ideas drive new projects, products, and strategies. In other words, we do more business together. One of the benefits of cross-functional teams, for example, is to increase proximity to people that work in far-flung departments connected by copper and glass wires.

In today's performing organization, everyone touches the marketplace. Customer-relationship management is no longer just the sales or service department's job. Those in previously internal functions such as Human Resources and Accounting must now be adept relationship managers beyond the four walls of the company as well. Had my insurance agency provider's "internal" procedures been linked to the customer-service function, I would have received the answers I sought right then and there. Lacking a good answer, a relationship-skill-trained customer rep would have assured me she would find out (and call me back!). Instead I was told, "We have a new system." OK, that's great—but for what end?

Effective relationship management throughout the organization avoids business failures such as this before they can start—partnerships, acquisitions, customer relations, and good business intelligence depend on it. Really successful people "surrender" to the call for customer intimacy. When we're dedicated to the success of our partners, employees, and customers, we learn how to blend our personal life with our work life. We will find a way and it will not feel an imposition, or a hassle. After all, we sell to people, not organizations. Integration, more than balance or compartmentalization, becomes our most newfound, successful strategy.

INFLUENCE FLOW

We live in a small world that's shrinking fast. Before the Internet, only five intermediaries on average were required to connect a relationship chain between any two people in the world. This came to be known as *six degrees of separation.* Now with the Internet this linkage principle may have dropped to four, or even three, degrees of separation. The World Wide Web increasingly disintermediates (shortens) our connections.

Relationship structures in today's organizational charts, as a result, no longer portray true influence flow. The reality of where real influence lies (and flows) remains hidden unless it is carefully mapped and the group dynamics is observed. The extent to which you inject your self into your work now determines your intimacy with, and therefore your influence over, colleagues, superiors, subordinates, and customers.

Of course, not all relationships are worth having or investing in and not all customers or employees are created equal. Each of us has only so much energy, so that phasing out unproductive or unprofitable relationships can be a good thing for everyone. Even though no one likes to be the bad guy and take on the job of firing someone, for example, this sometimes has to be done—for the good of an organization.

"If the person's not pulling his weight in a small company, it can affect the productivity of everybody else," business writer Richard Deems once explained to *Your Company* magazine. "People will think, 'Why are they keeping this person? And why am I doing his work?' Eventually they ask, 'Is this an effective organization or not?'"

Any company, large or small, will be only as good as its relationships. Companies with relationship cultures, as opposed to those with a deal culture, ultimately emerge with lower costs of doing business when their relationships are top-flight. Other benefits will include enhanced individual and organizational creativity, work-life distinction, and personal-life fulfillment. Over time, effective practice of PowerSkills can even drive momentum as others become invested in your success. As I observed while studying over 10,000 business leaders, this can become a hallmark of a professional life well spent.

A FRAMEWORK FOR TOP-OF-MIND SUCCESS

The PowerSkills of relationship management, then, represent a framework for personal and organizational success, wherever you may happen to be and whenever you might need them. They can permit individuals and companies to maintain an all-important top-of-mind visibility, that is, an awareness of you and/or your company foremost on the minds of your various relationships and connections. You are the first one they think of, you're the one they remember most easily, and the one accorded their highest esteem.

The five PowerSkills work in sequence to assure quality relationships:

1. POSITIONING

Here you establish the top-of-mind image you desire. Naturally, you do yourself no good creating an image that would not propel you toward your objectives. A sales expert, for example, wants to be recalled for her consultative sales expertise, not for how organized she keeps her office. An IT manager wants to be seen as someone who can solve user needs, not just an expert on technology.

Positioning refers to generating an image of yourself that will advance your business goals. When we position effectively, we communicate our added value, establishing credibility with, and in, the minds of those who matter.

2. HUNTING

Hunting refers to a process in which you identify and access the people with ideas, influence, and information that can benefit and add to your vision. Such valuable connections are your VIRs (very important relationships). As a hunter, you research needed resources outside of your immediate experience.

3. COACHING

Through *coaching* we build learning relationships with others as we deliver and exchange value. Creating value for others rewards you with a multiplier effect. When you assist others in attaining their professional goals, you create "value deposits," i.e., bank accounts of goodwill that you are later able to draw upon. Coaching makes business personal and reciprocal too; coaches often feel they've learned as much (or more!) than their coachees.

4. LEADING

If you've worked hard at the previous three stages, you've earned the right to approach others for help in achieving your objectives. *Leading* means motivating others to work with you to get things done that you want done. Here, others spend time helping you. The key is to lead your partners, prospects, and clients to victory, broadening their thinking and sharing a greater vision. This PowerSkill is used in conjunction with all the others, and you more effectively lead by influence.

5. FARMING

It's critical, when all is said and done, to maintain and harvest all that value you've long been creating and demonstrating. This takes planning and discipline but it pays off. *Farming* your communities of interest results in long term benefits for all. By keeping relationships current, relationship "farmers" till the soil for present and future value. They sow, they nurture—they reap!

Everyone has a relationship system whether they know it or not. Most of us, however, are so focused on tasks that we miss big opportunities that could come about from our relationships. The five PowerSkills you are about to explore in the next section of this book will help you evaluate and adjust your current relationship system and approach. More importantly, when you implement the PowerSkills, you will be building top-level relationships for bottom-line results.

CHAPTER KEY POINTS

▲ Relationships can be constructed, grown, fashioned, championed, fabricated, turned around, re-built, reborn, and materialized.

▲ Effective relationship management means: proactive, systematic development of strategic business relationships around trust, value and ongoing dialogue. R=T+V+D

▲ Know your customer well. Continuity begets consistency, which begets trust, instilling confidence both inside and outside an organization. Lou Gerstner had the right idea.

▲ Satisfaction from stakeholders can attain such levels that loyalty will hold even when the product or service temporarily slips to second place.

▲ The real work of an organization always gets done through relationship networks.

▲ Proximity beats similarity. Don't underestimate the value of face-to-face interaction.

▲ Effective relationship management throughout the organization avoids business failures before they can start.

▲ Companies with relationship cultures ultimately emerge with lower costs of doing business when their relationships are top flight.

▲ Everyone has a relationship system whether they know it or not, for better or for worse.

▲ The five PowerSkills (positioning, hunting, coaching, leading, farming) represent a framework for personal and organizational success permitting individuals and companies to maintain all-important Top-of-Mind visibility, and create value through truly collaborative relationships.

PART 2

POWERSKILLS

FOR

PERSONAL

LEADERSHIP

CHAPTER 4

POWERSKILL #1: POSITIONING

"Good business leaders create a vision, articulate the vision, passionately own the vision, and relentlessly drive it to completion."

—Jack Welch, CEO, General Electric

Visit website **www.homedepot.com** and you will encounter this message: "Your home, your home depot." Simple, warm, homey. With all its attendant Grow It, Fix It, Build It banners beckoning you, extending a hand to help with your home improvement needs, The Home Depot's home page assures you that you've arrived at a place where people will go out of their way to make you feel comfortable.

Starbucks has an interesting website too, an "artsy" one in particular. The slogan you find here reads, "Great coffee moments happen one customer, one partner, one cup at a time." Such a message sells us not just a cup of joe but an actual experience, specifically the sensation of being in one of their cafés and the added value that could come from it. Coffee? Yeah, sure. A chance to dream, and perhaps get started on a dream that soon makes it to reality and changes your life forever? Wow! This communication of an unexpected benefit from an international coffeehouse company is a powerful example of "positioning" at its best. By concentrating on an idea, a phrase, or a word, marketers position a definition of their company in your mind.

What happens when someone mentions Federal Express, the company that pioneered overnight delivery? "Absolutely, positively overnight!" that's what you think about. Or maybe you've taken in its latest positioning statement: "Over two million customers a day depend on FedEx for timely delivery of their packages and freight to locations worldwide." Two million! You have to have confidence when you hear this message, FedEx must be doing something right. Obviously, with two million customers each *day*, they have to be able to deliver what they promise.

We could go on and on: the Porsche website confidently says, "Welcome to the official Porsche Website" with a picture of a Carrera 4. A caption asks you to click on the language you want to read in and you think, "world-class" without it even needing to be said. American Airlines boasts: "The most popular airline site on the Web." Staples reminds you that it, and it alone, serves as "your online office manager."

All these companies are positioning themselves in their market-places, and indeed positioning is a term we associate with products and services as well as with companies and corporations. Just go to the website of any well-positioned company (our examples constitute only a scant few) and you will discover messages that reinforce the brand identity they wish to promote. With proper positioning, companies distinguish themselves from the mediocre sameness of the "pack."

Now let's get personal. What is *your* positioning? How are you perceived? Do people think of you as a true professional? An up-and-comer? A genuine, consistent winner?

Maybe you're thought of in other ways—trusted advisor, innovator, visionary, industry expert? How about team player? Tough negotiator? Entrepreneur? Dynamic leader? Professional manager?

You might also be thought of by what you do—QA manager, sales manager, accountant, consultant? Maybe your positioning has been negative, maybe how others perceive you causes you to wince: Has-been? Sloppy Joe? Time-waster? Whiner?

Like it or not, all of us at any moment in time are firmly positioned in the minds of those who know us. Our positioning and reputations are closely linked. This is particularly true if we have done nothing to actively position ourselves on our own, leaving the process to everyone else's active imaginations.

And remember, people have a lot of other things on their minds than you or your projects. Researchers tell us that the American adult is bombarded with over 3700 marketing messages every day from television, radio, books, magazines, e-mails, websites, faxes, voice messages, billboards, product packaging, advertisements on rented videos and even blimps flying overhead. How do you capture some mindshare in this environment?

Ask yourself this question: What is your "brand?" What image do you project? What picture forms in your customers' minds when they hear your or your company's name? How do they describe what you do for them? Once you have answered that one, ask yourself another one: Are you sure?

And this one: What is your "level of play?" How high up an organization's power structure do you interact? Whom do you influence—those on the bottom rungs of a corporate ladder or major players at the top?

Finally: Do people line up to invest themselves in your success? If you're paying attention to PowerSkill #1, they will at least be open to it.

If you position yourself effectively, as great business leaders do, you'll be able to achieve great things. Because it's so valuable, the very best leaders work hard to hone this skill to perfection. The good news here comes in two parts: (a) the positioning process itself is simple and straightforward, and (b) most of your competitors, for the most part, implement it poorly, if at all. So start by focusing on yourself and, for the moment at least, ignore the competition.

In establishing relationships, you never get a second chance to make a good first impression. Remember your mother saying, when you were going to a new school or joining a new group, "Don't worry, just be yourself and put your best foot forward," when sending you off on your own?

Yet have you ever noticed that when a relationship gets off to a poor start, and you quickly form a negative impression of someone, how difficult it is to turn around your own perceptions of and emotional reactions to that person? What is the likelihood of you providing your private feedback to that person if you don't want to be dealing with them often? Not likely, I'm sure you'll agree. Yet have you also noticed that with some relationships you start out at a high comfort level and it just keeps going up from there? That's why, like it or not, first (and most recent) impressions matter.

Whether introducing ourselves, communicating our ideas or just simply conducting business in general, we are constantly giving off signs and signals to those around us. Too often we're completely unaware of how these signs/signals are interpreted and can only approximate an educated guess as to what impressions they make. But we *can* make empirical observations of the effects of impressions we make and we can also ask for and pay attention to feedback from those who already know us. We are positioned in the minds of those with whom we have established relationships already.

Even after passing my fiftieth birthday, my Dad still calls me Jimmy, and that's fine for my family life. As we grow and develop ourselves in the business world, however, people's memories of us from an earlier stage of our development could end up hindering us, impeding our goals and our advancement.

Sometimes we must reposition ourselves with longtime colleagues, friends, and even family, or they might unwittingly hold us back.

The highest-achieving business leaders understand how important it is to establish credibility quickly in relationships. They realize that if they don't, they realize, fantastic opportunities can be lost forever. Yet I would venture a guess that most people in your present organization probably do not know how to effectively position themselves or the organization or its products and services. In that sense, unfortunately, they would be in an undesirable majority.

Most professional individuals seem to have little clue how to clearly present their own work, or their company's value proposition, in a compelling and concise way that reinforces the desired company image. Their tendency is to rely on the company's expensive marketing and advertising budgets, or on its public relations efforts, to position products and services (or the company's "brand") in the minds of customers.

For the business-to-business and professional services markets in particular, that is a very big mistake. Professionals in these areas are integral to the service and can largely create powerful word-of-mouth communication to constituents. Along with, or even as a substitute for, large-scale marketing efforts, a simple and concise message consistently delivered in daily interactions by single individuals can quickly establish their brand in the minds of current or potential customers.

Over the past 25 years, marketing gurus Jack Trout and Al Reis have taught us that the ultimate marketing battleground is *the mind*. The better we understand this, the more likely we are to understand how to position ourselves, our products, and services. Trout and Reis tell us that all minds are very busy, remembering only up to seven chunks of new information in each instance.

They also say that the ear controls the mind (that's why a "tag line" or "sound bite" is so important), that ears retain messages longer than eyes (say, after viewing a picture of your product), and that minds are emotional. Ultimately, it is futile to try to change people's minds. Trout and Reis suggest that products, companies, political candidates, individual professionals all have to "stand for" something if they want to achieve competitive advantage. Apply the knowledge of positioning—PowerSkill #1—and you'll begin to position yourself and stand for something in the relationships you engage in every day.

Most of us get easily turned off by the obviously insincere "masters of spin" found in politics and public relations, and get annoyed by the triumph of form over substance. The fact is that these folks are all practicing the art of positioning. Although positioning does not need to be carried out in a sleazy or disingenuous manner, it does need to be implemented. Why permit others to advance more quickly than you, positioning themselves and their ideas more effectively? This is an especially significant question if you feel you indeed possess the substance to go with the form. If you've truly got something to offer, why not market it effectively?

So positioning is not just for products and services, it's a PowerSkill that allows each one of us to clearly communicate our value, i.e., what we have to offer, to customers, prospects and colleagues. It will affect how successful we are in making an impact on our job, whether we advance or not, lead our profession, successfully promote our business or employer, even change careers, that is, reposition ourselves. Whatever our objective, we need to be ready for that initial impression we are going to make every time we meet someone new, answer our phone, introduce ourselves at a professional meeting, or send out an email.

DEVELOPING YOUR PERSONAL POSITIONING

My writing coach, Ken Lizotte, has published several books and hundreds of articles. He also helps thought leaders in diverse fields get their ideas published and attain visibility in the media. An unpretentious, very talented, and creative person, Ken also delivers very humorous keynote speeches.

One day, at an association meeting of small business executives, as everyone was getting up to briefly (and boringly) introduce themselves, it was Ken's turn. While everyone else got to describe themselves as someone who "works on IT problems" and who does "marketing consulting" or offers "accounting services to small businesses," Ken got up and announced, "My name is Ken Lizotte with Emerson Consulting Group in Concord Massachusetts and I make people famous! I do this by providing writing and media services to consulting firms and to professional speakers." He left the audience with a question: "How famous are you among your target market and how much more famous would you like to be?"

Needless to say, Ken got everyone's attention, not to mention hordes of potential customers that swarmed around him during the break. Are your introductions, or what I call your "impact messages," that effective? If not, you've got some work to do. You'll be pleased to know that, just as Ken did, you can learn how relatively easy it is and get yourself properly positioned in no time. Now, let's look at how you can design your own impact statements.

There are several ways to formulate your own impact message (and statements). One is to sketch out about twenty or thirty definition statements of whatever you are trying to position, i.e., you, your product, your idea, your company. Next circle twelve key words you find in all of them that seem to best describe it. You can then draw your positioning message or tag line from those twelve words.

EXAMPLE: Ken originally circled such words as "notoriety," "fame," "celebrity," "visibility," "marketability." The one that seemed to ring truest was "visibility," but in thinking about it, "fame" was accurate too, although not a term typically used in business. Yet precisely because of that, Ken chose "famous" in order to jar everyone to attention when they heard him say it, to "hook" them so they'd listen to the rest of his statement, and to stand out from the usual bland, run-of-the-mill deliveries. Once he tried it, it worked splendidly. Now he had a positioning message that truly set him apart not only from his competitors but from his peers as well. A brand is a promise and Ken delivers on his brand.

Another way to formulate your impact message might be to brainstorm about twenty-five skills you bring to the marketplace by thinking about what value your clients most appreciate about you. Having whipped such a list together, circle or underline those skills you feel most accurately reflect your true talents. If it helps, ask yourself these key questions: What do I bring to the marketplace? What satisfaction have I produced for my customers? What problems have I solved?

Once you've narrowed down all your ideas to a manageable level, crossing off those of lesser impact, circling or underlining others that seem strongest, you will soon be able to zero in on the highest value you bring and start to focus your message and craft your hook.

EXAMPLE: Chris Roberts, a former colleague and computer sales manager turned CEO, had an unusual method of getting his sales reps to master this skill. Typically, at the start of a sales staff meeting, Chris would tell everyone to share with everyone else in the room why their prospective customers should buy the company's products. Chris didn't merely request that everyone take a stab at this, however. He insisted that they do so while holding a lighted match. You can bet that each of his sales reps learned how to concisely define the value of their product lines in 30 seconds or less. More than one scorched forefinger and thumb preceded such practice sessions but the end-results overall were pretty impressive.

Note that the structure of your impact statements are critical. You want to be brief and to the point, beginning with a concise "hook" that is also provocative (like Ken's—"I make people *famous!*"), and that next clearly communicates whom you serve (client base) and how you serve them (value added). It should also end with a question or a suggestive comment that invites the listener to want to learn more about your service and/or take action. Ken's, you recall, ends this way: "I would leave you with this question: How famous are you among your target market, and how much more famous would you like to be?" A listener must wonder, upon hearing this, if there is more that he or she could be doing to increase his/her market visibility, and as a result, as Ken implies, gain more fame.

To help you shape an effective, bottom-line results-oriented impact statement consider the two examples on the following page.

While this seems formulaic for practice purposes, experiment with different approaches, hooks and closes. Keep in mind your objective for the impact statement, your audience, and context. Your objective may be a powerful introduction, an invitation to discuss an important issue or get a quick decision made. Each objective will require a different approach and close.

Think for a moment about people you most remember at the last company where you worked, or for that matter from your high school or college. Who do you remember most?

Now think about what it is you remember about them. Can you see them, hear their voices, and recall what they said or did? Ask yourself what is the *single thing* you most remember about them? Is there one word you can summon to best describe their way of being with others?

▶ EXAMPLE 1 External Introduction

Greeting:	Hello, I'm Dawn Jacobson and I'm COO at White Plains Engineering.
Hook:	We keep our clients' computer networks up and running and we make sure their people know exactly what to do when something goes wrong.
Client Base:	Our clients are financial services companies including banks and brokerages.
Value Added:	This past year our reliability teams completely eliminated down time for clients with this requirement.
Close:	How is down time currently impacting or costing your organization?

▶ EXAMPLE 2 Internal Introduction

Greeting:	Hello, I'm Jack Jones with the quiet professionals in Accounting.
Hook:	My group keeps all your paychecks coming out on time and answering your benefit and tax questions.
Client Base:	We work for all of you, with any payroll issues you may have.
Value Added:	This past year we added three new benefit programs and provided the self-service capability that allows you to choose your own options.
Close:	I'm here today to learn how you want to take advantage of these new features.

When I did this exercise myself, I remembered a fellow I would describe as "aggressive," a gal I'd call "generous," a friend from high school (still a friend now) I'd label "funny," and a former colleague I'd have to call "self-serving." These are emotionally based reactions that we retain through all the years that go by, in essence the *feeling* we had about each individual. This is also that person's positioning in our minds. Capture that one (positive) quality about yourself and use it to cut through information overload.

GET SOME FEEDBACK ON YOUR POSITIONING

How do people remember *you*? Do you know? How are people seeing you *now*? I'm talking about customers, clients, prospects, and influencers as well as colleagues and friends. After giving a talk ("Positioning Your Services for Maximum Value") to the Institute for Management Consultants, I was approached by several experienced business advisors who each expressed to me the desire to advance his/her practice to the next level. "I'd like to charge higher fees," one said, "and eventually add more people to my organization. But I'm having trouble differentiating my firm."

In one case, an organizational consultant came forward with a colleague, a reasonably successful sales consultant. Though both had busy practices, neither's business was growing very quickly anymore. Both sensed they could be getting business from current customers but that their clients saw their skills as too narrow and therefore didn't think of them for certain types of projects.

I suggested they pair off and perform an inventory for each other on client satisfaction. Being in non-competitive practice areas but with similar categories of clients, each went ahead to design and conduct a confidential client and colleague survey for the other, examining clients' perception of capability, value, service delivery, and weaknesses. You could say that this was similar to what is now known as a 360-degree feedback process—getting some confidential, aggregated feedback from multiple sources in your circle of activity.

When the final reports came in, both sets of eyes opened wide. Though relatively self-aware individuals, each nonetheless registered genuine surprise at how many of their customers viewed them. Some surprises were pleasant, some frank and tough. One of the biggest surprises for both, a happy one, was that their clients didn't feel they charged enough for the value these clients felt they received. On a less jubilant note, both sets of clients revealed they would love to receive more contact from their consultant and they wouldn't mind being asked the kinds of questions that might lead to more varied assignments (and hence more business for each consultant).

This short bit of research led each to develop a communication plan that would leverage their perceived strengths with current clients as well as prospects. They didn't waste time trying to overcome perceived weaknesses, i.e., changing individual clients' minds, but they did improve certain processes that seemed to annoy their clients. This 360-degree feedback research forced each to take aim at their added value and sharpen it in new ways. As a result, their businesses improved as they added new services to existing clients and began behaving differently, more proactively, and more interactively. The sales expert even ended up repositioning himself among current clients and both found ways to position themselves more clearly in the minds of new prospects.

So if you're having trouble coming up with just the right impact message, perhaps finding a partner, as these two consultants did, and researching each other's client list will help you define your value and adjust its context correctly.

CREATING TOP-OF-MIND AWARENESS (TOMA)

Keep this formula in mind:
7 x 7 x 7 = TOMA

The three *sevens* in this formula indicate how to create top-of-mind awareness in a business relationship. It takes seven *touches* to gain meaningful awareness with an executive, or for that matter, with another individual in any setting. Moreover, research suggests each touch should be spaced, on average, at *seven-week intervals* and it will typically take *seven relationships* in all, within a given organization, to make an impact on this organization and to keep that impact alive. Seven relationships, seven touches each, seven times a year if you want to win or maintain a great account or business partner. This takes some forethought, a plan, and follow-through.

The fact is that, in business, it isn't only whom you know but who knows you. Take your VIRs, for example, that is, your very important relationships—clients, superiors, partners, suppliers, administrators, and so on. If you aren't top of mind with them, you'll certainly miss many, desirable opportunities. Worse, when you need to reach your VIRs, you won't be able to—they'll be out, they'll get back to you, they'll be tied up. But by creating the right impression initially, through an impact message that clearly delivers your distinctive value, and then reinforcing it with "added-value communications," you will generate a level of top-of-mind awareness that will suit your business development needs.

A Lesson from Hollywood

Nowhere else in the world will you find more shameless self-promotion than in Hollywood, California during the weeks immediately preceding the Academy Awards. It is commonplace for both nominees and Oscar wannabes to take out full-page advertisements in *Variety*, the *Hollywood Reporter* and other industry trade publications in order to attain the highest visibility during the evaluation process. At the 71st annual awards ceremony, for example, March, 1999, Roberto Benigni won the category of "Best Actor in a Lead Role" for his performance in the movie "Life is Beautiful" *(La Vita E Bella)*. Only the second person in Academy history to win while acting in a foreign language film, Benigni joined Sophia Loren who did it in 1961 for her performance in the movie "Two Women."

But Benigni's success begs a question: How could a little-known Italian comedian from the tiny Tuscan village of Misericordia suddenly rise from obscurity to invite comparisons (as has been the case) with the comic genius Charlie Chaplin?

And a second question: Would you ever predict that a film about the Holocaust made by an Italian comedian (he was also director and co-writer) would earn such acclaim internationally, launching his career to unimagined heights? If you saw him in this movie, I'm sure you'd agree his performance is simply unforgettable.

Now remember that other nominees are shelling out big bucks to publicists and for ads in trade papers and Benigni, in contrast, simply comes to Hollywood, steps out on the town with Liz Taylor and Rod Steiger, getting his photo with each of them plastered across every media channel possible. Since Elizabeth Taylor and Rod Steiger remain major "brands" in moviegoers' minds, the association with them instantly *positions* Benigni as a world-class candidate for the upcoming Oscar. You've heard of course of guilt by association? Well, fame by association works, too. Who you hang with has lots to do with how well (or ill) you get positioned.

TOOTING ANOTHER'S HORN

How else can you create significant top-of-mind awareness (TOMA)? This one's amazingly easy, yet all too frequently (sad to say) completely ignored. Give people credit. That's right, just give other people credit for what gets accomplished on your watch, or for what they do, with or without you, or for what they've accomplished in their past. Help someone else look good even by suggesting a great idea privately and then letting them take all the credit for it. Perform such generous, egoless acts, letting others reap the benefits and kudos of accomplishments and great ideas, and magical things will begin happening for you as well. What goes around, comes around.

Cognitive dissonance created in others by giving them more than you yourself are getting or by recognizing them more than you reference yourself typically pays the "creditor" with invaluable dividends of good will. Most people, in hating to toot their own horn, also miss out on the flip side, the power derived from recognizing others. The reality is that when you unselfishly help and recognize others, your reputation soars. Such recognition is inexpensive, efficient and powerfully effective. It is also remarkably underutilized, considering its great power. Capable of building trust, confidence, good will (great will!) and loyal relationships, tooting other people's horns will enable you to celebrate differences you find while implementing other PowerSkills (such as hunting and coaching). It will also bolster your own TOMA with these and other relationships in the process.

CAUTION: DON'T GET STEREOTYPED

Reinventing, that is, repositioning yourself, can be hard to do. The world wants to put us in a box and keep us there; life is more comfortable that way. Let individuals break out of their box, and courageously blaze new trails, with all its ups, downs, wins, losses, uncertainties, and everybody else might be called upon one day to do the same. For many individuals, this is not a picture of joyful living.

Remember when Arnold Schwarzenegger was known primarily as a bodybuilder? Most of us actually do not, Arnold's notoriety at that time being much more limited. In repositioning himself as an actor, he was of course relegated to muscle roles initially—Conan the Barbarian, Commando, The Terminator. Who could see Mr. Universe as anything more than a muscle-bound action hero? In fact, in Arnold's earliest movie, which practically nobody saw, he was paired with Arnold Stang, a puny, bespectacled comic actor from the fifties and sixties, and Schwarzenegger's stage name at the time, created by his agents, was (are you ready?) "Arnold Strong."

Determined and willing to take risks, Arnold eventually broke out of this stereotype, repositioning himself as a comic actor in his own right. Consider his non-Conan, non-Terminator films: "Twins" with Danny DeVito, "Kindergarten Cop," "Junior" (Arnold gets pregnant), "Jingle All the Way." By keeping at it, taking roles producers initially did not want to give him, working hard, keeping his chin up, he finally broke through to the mega-star he is today.

Now when there's a movie Arnold wants to be in, you can be sure, if they can pay his twenty-plus million fee, he *will* be in it!

Be willing to take the risk of bringing who you are into your work. Sooner or later, if you are persistent enough, you will be perceived multidimensionally. That can mean being perceived as a person with many interests and talents not easily categorized by just your job role. Your positioning becomes one of character with many talents, not narrow skillsets, and this positioning will be far more potent and memorable. You command higher compensation as your perceived value creates greater customer demand in the marketplace.

DON'T BE A ONE-NOTE PLAYER

The alleyways of corporate America are littered with once-mighty behemoths that refused to change horses in the middle of a fast-moving, global marketplace. For this reason, you've also got to remember to position yourself in a manner that allows for change and flexibility as the need arises.

Digital Equipment Corporation (DEC) comes to mind first, a gigantic industry leader for many years and one of only a dozen or so companies prominently profiled in the 1983 best seller *In Search of Excellence*. Yet only ten years later, the king began to falter because it wouldn't depart from its principle product of many years, the so-called minicomputer.

As the nineties began, consumers clamored louder and louder for smaller-sized personal computers but the earlier words of DEC's founder, Ken Olson, still reverberated like a church bell on Sunday inside his upper management's ears. "There's no reason," Olsen had once proclaimed, "anyone would have any use for a computer in their home." So the DEC brand is no more, its once-proud horse and buggy sadly stranded in the middle of the Assabet River, a swift-running stream that gushes on through its former main campus.

Being flexible and adaptive to change is essential for individuals as well. Going beyond what we know and are comfortable with can, however, make us feel vulnerable. As individuals, we are multidimensional and have many potentialities, capabilities, and interests. Our activities and our positioning must be flexible enough for others to see us in multiple contexts or we can easily be marginalized. Actually, our openness to change and new learning turns our willingness to be vulnerable into an asset. Show your vulnerability from time to time and watch what happens. I predict communication and trust channels will open up in a way that surprises you and offers you something of value in return.

Everybody makes mistakes, but hiding them constantly, always showing our "business face" as a uniform causes others to not fully trust us or recognize that we are growing and evolving.

VALUES CONNECT OR CLASH

Your positioning is also tied to your values and sometimes we take our personal values for granted. You will notice that effective leaders sprinkle their values into their impact statements to reinforce what they stand for. Analyzing where you connect and clash with others can help you to pinpoint your core values that you will include in your personal communications.

> **EXHIBIT 4.1 Values Checklist**

Accomplishment	Honesty
Commitment	Integrity
Competence	Justice
Confidence	Learning
Contribution	Lifestyle
Cooperation	Objectivity
Courage	Openness
Creativity	Peace of Mind
Credibility	Personal Growth
Curiosity	Positive Attitude
Diversity	Productivity
Drive	Professionalism
Enthusiasm	Punctuality
Family	Quality
Financial Security	Recognition
Flexibility	Reliability
Forthrightness	Relationships
Free Time	Respect
Friendship	Responsiveness
Frugality	Sense of Urgency
Generosity	Simplicity
Genuineness	Spirituality
Happiness	Vision
Health	

We also want to determine our very important relationships by thinking about who we know with values consistent with our own. Important partnerships work best with people that share your core values. But examining your relationships from the other side works too. Whose values clash with yours? Whose values do you abhor? Who do you wish you never had to deal with?

Determining opposite values, i.e., the "triggers" that set you off and start you running in the opposite direction, can help you more clearly identify those that are meaningfully yours. Think about your relationships on all fronts and notice which ones you find distasteful or annoying.

EXERCISE:

Use the Values Checklist of Exhibit 4.1, on the previous page, to examine your key values. Check off those that are most meaningful for you. The next time you are having a conflict with someone, consult this checklist of values to find out why you are clashing. Remember that values are at the heart of connections or clashes with others and are likely to be an expression of your own core values. Use words that reflect your core values as part of your positioning and impact messages. Recall the two impact message examples in this chapter—"professionals" and "reliability " were core values worked into the messages.

CREATING THE BUZZ FACTOR

In the second half of the nineties, we heard the term "buzz" thrown about a lot. Buzz is positioning in action in the informal human network. Here are some of the *building blocks of buzz* along with familiar examples.

As you read about them, ask yourself how you might apply each principle to yourself, your company, your team, a current project. Examples of each element could inspire you to a similar "buzz strategy."

▲ **BE PROVOCATIVE.** Celebrity attorney/author Alan Dershowitz comes to mind here, always taking a hard stand on things, often unpopularly so. He never hesitates to make statements that shock and exasperate. One of his many books was even titled, "Chutzpah."

▲ **ADOPT A MEMORABLE NAME.** Roth IRAs, beanie babies, JFK— Enough said?

▲ **REMEMBER THE BENEFITS OF GREAT TIMING.** George Burns once said the most important segments of an act were the beginnings and the ends. The middle, ah, people rarely remembered that part, he insisted, but start them off with a firecracker and leave them laughing as you go off and you'd always create a lasting impression.

▲ **RUMOR CAN CREATE A BUZZ.** Broadway producer David Merrick used to nail this one. Whenever he opened a new play, he'd always make ticket-holders wait outside until the doors opened at least 45 minutes late. As more and more patrons arrived, the line would begin to stretch down the street. Even if the play had only sold a small number of tickets, a buzz on the street would go out that people were lining up in droves to get it in and see this new play. Next night, typically Merrick's play would sell out.

▲ **THE INSIDE STORY STIRS INTEREST.** Trading stocks over the Internet seems to exemplify this one. Once a rumor goes out over the email-waves, a company's fortune can be made, or broken, in minutes or hours.

▲ **SCARCITY BREEDS RESPECT.** I met a professional speaker who, whenever he's received messages from meeting planners who are thinking of booking him for an upcoming conferences, makes it a point to return the calls, if possible, from an airport. Even if he's not traveling, he sometimes goes out of his way to get to the nearest noisy terminal and do his business development calls.

"That way I can say," he told me, "'Hello, yeah, I'm calling you from the airport.'" Busy, popular speakers, after all, spend half their lives hanging out in busy airports.

▲ EMPLOY THE RING OF TRUTH. A former colleague, Lucio Vollaro, is a top executive search consultant in Milan. Known widely as someone who knows virtually every top technology CEO in Europe, Lucio regularly attends industry conferences where he always goes right up to a keynote speaker (usually an industry-leading CEO) after his or her presentation, compliments the speaker, then requests an electronic version of the presentation slides. Over the course of the next week, while meeting with his prospects, Lucio then will casually comment that he met recently with the CEO of XYZ Company who had a few relevant things to say about the prospect's market. He then flips open his laptop and shares with them his "new colleague's" latest thinking on the matter.

▲ WHAT IS YOUR AUDIENCE TODAY, TOMORROW? We offer many facets to others in various segments of our lives. We express ourselves somewhat differently with our boss than with our colleagues, with our spouses than with our children, with our hairdresser than with our landlord. Each individual in our lives represents, in a sense, a totally different audience. Tailoring how we position ourselves can ensure maximum and appropriate value exchange for all concerned.

KEEPING A POWERSKILLS JOURNAL

You can help yourself develop your PowerSkills if you start taking notes along the way and enter your thoughts in a "PowerSkills Journal." Recording your reactions, insights, milestones and even contacts in a dedicated journal can synthesize what you learn and help you make some sense out of it. You can also record what you have trouble with, to remind yourself to keep working on it and/or note the progress you make.

CHAPTER KEY POINTS

▲ Like it or not, all of us at any moment in time are firmly positioned in the minds of those who know us.

▲ By effectively positioning themselves, their teams, their products and their companies, business leaders can build a following.

▲ A majority of professionals seem clueless about how to clearly or powerfully present their own work, or their company's value proposition, in a compelling and concise way that reinforces the desired company image.

▲ Be willing to take risks to bring who you are into your work, and who you want to be, and your positioning will become one of character not narrow skillsets, far more potent and memorable.

▲ Determining opposite values, i.e., "triggers," can help you clearly identify those values that are meaningfully yours and that can be reinforced in your impact and positioning statements.

▲ Sometimes we must reposition ourselves with longtime colleagues, friends, and even family, or they might unwittingly hold us back.

▲ A simple and concise message consistently delivered in daily interactions by single individuals can quickly establish brand in the minds of current or potential customers.

▲ Who you associate with has a lot to do with how you are positioned.

▲ By giving credit to others, and tooting their horn, you create good will that helps to position you positively in people's minds.

▲ If you want to have an impact quickly in a new organization, create the right buzz—there is a way to do it.

QUESTIONS FOR YOUR POWERSKILLS JOURNAL

Here and at the end of each of the next four chapters, I'll offer you some relevant questions to consider. Try to reflect on these questions before going on to the next chapter. If you stretch yourself to really think about PowerSkills, you'll soon be practicing them with regularity and relative ease.

▲ What is your brand?

▲ Are you top of mind with the influencers in your field?

▲ Are you moving your ideas successfully through your organization and networks?

▲ Are you fully recognized for your skillsets and your added value?

▲ Have you invoked full cooperation for your projects?

▲ Have you created or reinforced a sense of excitement for your team and company?

PRACTICE TIPS

▲ Develop and practice three personal impact messages for different internal and external audiences.

▲ Volunteer for a 360-degree feedback analysis to test your personal brand, the strengths for you to exploit, and the areas to improve.

RESOURCES

Click on **www.powerskills.com/positioning** for books, links, and resources to develop the positioning PowerSkill.

How to Get Your Point Across in 30 Seconds or Less by Milo O. Frank. London, Corgi Books, 1986. ISBN 0-671-72752-4

The New Positioning: The Latest on the World's #1 Business Strategy by Jack Trout with Steve Rivkin. New York, McGraw-Hill Book Company, 1996. ISBN 0-07-065328-3

Words That Sell: The Thesaurus to Help You Promote Your Products, Services, and Ideas by Richard Bayan. Chicago: Contemporary Books, 1984. ISBN 0-8092-4799-2

CHAPTER 5

POWERSKILL #2: HUNTING

"There is a passion for hunting something deeply implanted in the human breast."

—Charles Dickens

When you hear the word "hunter," what pictures come up in your mind? Buffalo Bill raging on horseback alongside ten thousand bisons, blasting round after round from his Springfield into the herd and hooping it up each time one of the big bully critters falls?

Or maybe it's Daniel Boone unloading his musket at a deer, not for cruel sport, of course, but for food—not too many Safeways out there in the Kentucky woods in those days!

How about Davy Crockett ("kilt him a b'ar when he was only three"), eighteenth century French trappers in Canada, or Native Americans tracking down antelope?

Of course, hunting does not have to connote chasing wild

animals and killing them for food (or sport). Explorers, for example, are hunters. Lewis and Clark hunted for years for the Northwest Passage, Columbus in his voyages had been hunting for the New World, Amelia Earhart hunted for new air travel routes all around the world.

For that matter, we could even call inventors "hunters." Wasn't Einstein hunting for something when he dreamed up all kinds of wild-eyed scientific ideas? Was Marie Curie hunting as she embarked on yet another chemistry experiment? Bucky Fuller in his quest for a better use of space (finally "found" in his conceptualization of the geodesic dome)? Marconi? Copernicus? Guttenberg?

In business too, there are hunters. Like their counterparts in the scientific and explorer realms, business hunters are seekers of value, possibilities, excitement, and new opportunities. The smartest business hunters maintain their perspective by framing this PowerSkill as a game, knowing too that the outcome of such sport can yield serious rewards for its winners. Consider, for example, those professionals in our society who are extraordinarily compensated for what they do:

▲ The entrepreneur who devises a new way of meeting customer needs

▲ The missionary sales executive in search of early customers for a new product

▲ The corporate manager who successfully identifies acquisition targets for the company's growth

▲ The recruiter who seeks out and finds top industry talent

▲ The law partner who unfailingly brings in the biggest clients

▲ The venture investor that finds and funds, tomorrow's economic stars

In all these cases, whatever their instincts about hunting, at some point in their careers, these individual professionals learned to hunt. What's more, they likely enjoyed (and still enjoy) the *thrill* of the hunt.

It's easy to spot the hunters in every business organization. Action-oriented questioners, they like speaking and listening at a high data rate and usually have several exciting things going on concurrently. They are highly curious, not afraid to try new things or get out of their comfort zones, and, even though always very busy, can be surprisingly accessible and communicative.

Highly organized, though sometimes mysteriously so, they have a methodical approach to their work. They make more outbound calls than others in their respective organizations and typically adapt quickly to technology when they sense it would be useful. By and large, they bring a sense of humor and an energetic flow to their work and can get so focused that they lose all track of time.

While very focused on their targets, hunters nonetheless keep themselves open to new ideas and methods, embracing collaboration while they juggle lots of relationships. Hunters are also typically self confident in the knowledge that if they don't know the answer to something they can find people or places to turn to quickly. Obviously very proactive, they stimulate their organizations to be proactive as well.

Contrary to popular opinion, hunting is not the exclusive domain of sales professionals. Since today everyone in a top-performing organization must interact with its customers, being effective means developing strong both internal and external knowledge for use as windows to one's industry. For example, the modern CFO needs to be attuned to the trends in the marketplace as she will often get involved in sourcing everything from new information systems to technology licensing to capital equipment to financial instruments. Today's CFO is increasingly a relationship-smart "deal maker" (or "deal breaker") in major contracts with business partners.

"We got rid of the title 'division controller' here because it sends the wrong message, that finance is a roadblock that must be passed through or around," Leonard Purkis, CFO of Iomega Corporation, told CFO magazine in a June 1997 cover story about the growing involvement of CFOs in marketing, selling, and strategic planning.

The article tells the story of how Iomega's finance department actually helped save the company from a potentially disastrous Christmas season due to a shortfall in the company's stock of its new computer zip-drives. An advertising campaign had been budgeted, commercials produced, and TV airtime reserved. But no way, manufacturing announced, could we keep up with anticipated demand should the ad campaign succeed.

Rather than nixing the whole project, a more traditional finance division's response, Howard Maymon, then finance director of business analysis, suggested that marketing expenditures go on, but tapped instead for the company's higher-end products, its Jaz drive and Ditto tape drive. The happy result was that Jaz and Ditto got an "unexpected year-end marketing boost," CFO reported, and the Zip-drive promotion was shelved until the spring when stocks were fully available.

"Everyone in finance, from the CFO on down, has to send the message that finance helps drive sales," Purkis says at the end of the article, "and we do that by partnering with the business units." CFOs then may no longer function as roadblocks to growth but prime players on the front lines of customer value.

HUNTERS ARE MADE, NOT BORN

Although we all tend to sort out our vocations and choices of professional work based upon our various personal interests in people, ideas, data, or things, every one of us has the potential to develop this PowerSkill; it's merely a matter of focusing your energies that way. From recruiters to college professors to research librarians to art collectors, upon investigation, you will find every time that the most successful in each category are its hunters. Anthropologists may argue that men have always been more disposed to hunting than women (our so-called "gatherers"), yet in my 30 years of business experience, I have never observed an obvious gender gap in hunting skills.

This is especially true now in the Information Age when the kind of hunting we do requires sifting through information and building and drawing upon relationships. In light of that, it may be that women have, in fact, a decided advantage. So many are in knowledge-worker positions today, that, when coupled with their possibly innate proclivity toward relationship management, women would seem to appear better equipped than men in this area. In contrast, the more traditional male tendencies to go it alone and keep knowledge private, i.e., to "keep one's cards close to the vest," can hamper many men's opportunities in this regard and as a result their potential.

The good news, however, is that hunting, no matter how strongly affected by innate talent or cultural conditioning, can be learned. Some of the best business leaders admit that hunting did *not* come naturally to them, they had to learn it, but that once they did, its value in their professional lives proved enormous. So hunters, including the most successful ones, are by and large made, not born, raising hope for all of us.

FINDERS, MINDERS AND GRINDERS

In so many firms, particularly professional services ones, the division of labor consistently provides maximum rewards for "finders," those partners whose job it is to hunt and "bring in the work." "Minders," on the other hand, are associates and junior partners who service clients on a day-to-day basis, whereas "grinders" are researchers, staff professionals, and administrative people who grind out the technical work, often with limited (if any) client contact. Though lucrative for the hunters at the top, this model can ultimately destroy an organization and its level of client service. Retention of staff often becomes focused upon aggressive compensation for the top hunter-performers while the rest of the organization starves for meaningful work.

The problem here is not so much the division of labor but the lack of tight integration of the client teams geared around client needs. Communication suffers too, as does organization-wide learning. Yet the opposite approach can be extremely satisfying for both clients and associates. When talented minders and grinders acquire client development and management skills, the investment of educational effort pays off in client retention and other bottom-line dividends.

As a firm owner and Managing Partner for Fenwick Partners, a national retained executive search firm, I was focused upon growth. Yet my frustration ran high as I sought quality experienced professionals for my company and few could be found. While putting together a training program, I developed a process, after considerable trial and error, to teach professionals from other industries how to do executive recruiting, i.e., how to hunt.

Every field has its methodology, whether hunters are picking stocks, arranging acquisitions, or providing technical solutions. The best practitioners develop their own rules of thumb, usually variants of the scientific method for that particular field. The real nuggets of insight, however, often derive from the interactive discussions of the process during "mentoring" of associates. That's why formalizing a "best practices" methodology requires some vision on the part of business leaders, and some preparation. Otherwise valuable knowledge in the organization will not be captured before these best practitioners move upward and onward, failing to leave behind their gold.

Most firms simply fail to incorporate these "best practices" into a structured training program and so they are lost. In essence, this is the promise of software-based "knowledge management" programs, which my colleagues in management consulting, market research, and corporate training hope will be the ultimate solution. With knowledge management becoming such a big industry today, software developers are going all-out to find ways to link business processes to actual behavior, retaining it and passing it on.

The challenge, of course, is that knowledge today constantly finds itself upstaged by newer knowledge. Remember the model globe you had as a kid? Even the ones made only year or two ago fall out of date as new nations get formed. In such a world, it's not always easy to rely solely on computerized knowledge systems. For whatever system we use, knowledge ultimately must connect to real people who unfortunately are not always consistently connected to the system nor have the incentive to keep the system up-to-date. For that reason, it's frequently a lot easier, despite our technological world, to make a couple of phone calls to just the right people to get an answer to a complex business question than to surf the Internet, scan a database, or even visit the corporate (or public) library.

On the other hand, such resources prove invaluable for certain types of research. In the end, a hunter in any field needs to know how to do both—collaborative networking with real, live people for primary-source-based research as well as "secondary" research with available public databases, information archives, or other inanimate sources.

THE HUNTER'S SEARCH METHODOLOGY

Sad to say, it's been my experience that most business people are poorly equipped to do either type of research, primary or secondary. This, of course, will affect their ability to make informed decisions, gain important business intelligence, know their customers, recruit a team or determine the right strategy. But experienced hunters understand they must constantly weigh the balance between process and the bottom line. Too little preparation and process, they will tell you, can deliver a decidedly inferior result while too much process makes everything cumbersome and slow. The mark of the seasoned hunter then is the capacity to make keen judgments quickly on process changes as new information is gained. At the end of the day, hunters know that speed (cycle time), ethics (values), and quality (of end result) are what matter most.

The following is a template of any good hunter's search process. Skipping any of these nine steps weakens the result. We will use the job hunt analogy to describe the process. By adopting and practicing these steps, you can significantly advance your prowess in hunting, PowerSkill #2.

1. VISUALIZE!

First form a mental picture of your desired end result and answers you seek for the Who, What, When, Why and How of your hunt. Suppose you've decided it's time to change your employer, but you wonder where you can take your talents and experience, who would want your developed expertise. Sit down, reflect, and imagine what you'd love to find. Picture the kind of workplace you'd like to next be in, the kind of work you'd be asked to do, the feeling you get from your new boss, from colleagues, from customers you would be dealing with. Picture it all clearly—it's the first step to getting there.

2. SIZE UP THE TERRITORY.

What's the "big" picture, the macro view? Where are the big game? The best opportunities? Consider industry structure, demographics, market drivers, and influencers. What constitutes the strong and weak factors in your hunt, and the formidable forces? When looking for a job, learn the field without regard to "who's hiring" and "who's not hiring." In your hunters' mind, they're all hiring if the candidate is you.

3. KNOW YOUR TARGET'S ASSOCIATIONS AND BEHAVIORS.

True hunters know, when shopping for a new job, it's not enough to simply do a little research over the Web and know the basic business health of your prospective new employer. What's the company's culture like as well? What's the personality type of your potential new boss? What are this company's goals for the future and what relationships has it been using to get there? What industry or professional groups do its managers belong to?

Search out all facets of your potential new employer's ways of doing things and you'll know exactly how well you're likely to fit in.

4. **ORGANIZE YOUR SEARCH TEAM.**

Formally or informally, who might have expert input or could get invested in your success? Brainstorm your strategy and project plan with your "search party." What tools and resources can we use? Where should we get started? When? Print and distribute the plan. Are there persons in your relationship data base who can introduce you to employees of your target company? Are there persons in your relationship database who are employed by the company themselves? You won't know who can help you until you profile those you currently know.

5. **DEFINE SPECIFICATIONS AND REQUIREMENTS.**

Get input from your search team and prioritize the "must haves" of your hunt and the "nice to haves." For job hunts, make a list of what you want your next employer to look like. You can draw on step 1, the visualization that kicked the process off.

6. **CONDUCT INITIAL RESEARCH AND TEST SAMPLE RESULT(S).**

By testing sample results against your requirements, you may fine-tune your strategy. The methods you choose and their possible results will scale up or down, based upon your initial research. Doing a few interviews at companies that you may not want to work for, for example, may help you fine-tune what you eventually want to find.

7. **COMPLETE THE MAJORITY OF YOUR RESEARCH EFFORT.**

So often the best solutions come in the last 20 percent of the research effort. Avoid a natural temptation to stop mining if the process gets too easy, or too tough. Of course, a great early solution may come along too, so keep alert! But keep looking for the best answer (in the case of a job hunt, for your "ideal" employer) right up until the end of your previously determined time frame.

8. SECURE THE BEST SOLUTION.

For this step, compare all solutions found to your initial requirements. This helps you recognize the best overall solution. Comparing the choices against each other rather than each against the requirements can become a zero-sum game without advancing yourself. Reference the candidate choices thoroughly for your very best final choice. What "short lists" have you come up with of employer candidates who appear to be "ideal"?

9. THANK YOUR SOURCES AND SHARE LESSONS LEARNED.

Input reusable data (often forgotten or ignored), then thank and reward your sources, and debrief your search team. After much disciplined and supervised practice on many projects, this process will become your standard modus operandi. Congratulations! You found the ideal new job. Others will rejoice in the telling of successful hunt details, which will invariably be instructive and interesting. Share what you've done and recount what you've learned with style.

HOW BIG IS YOUR SANDBOX?

Hunters consistently expand their spheres of influence over time, building a network that respects their value, achievements, and opinions. This process results in a great deal of personal and professional growth as deeper and wider relationship and knowledge banks are established, pushing out the borders of what I call your business relationship "sandbox." As the youngest son of a blue-collar family growing up in a small farming community in the fifties, I hardly expected to be interacting daily with world-renowned heads of multinational corporations and investment firms by my middle thirties. Nor did I expect to be serving clients on multiple continents in so many diverse industries.

Yet my experiences are commonplace today, especially for those willing to accept challenging roles in the fastest-growing sectors of their industry. Such roles stretch one's capabilities. The addition of a few lucky breaks and right assignments, with a good mentor or two thrown in along the way, can make all the difference.

The majority of people are so focused on their daily drill that they fail to even recognize such vast opportunities all around them. They are unwittingly "Not Open for Business," largely by not opening their eyes to the magical possibilities of new relationships.

Several years ago, my son Jason, then age ten, remarked to me that "Most grown-ups don't have many friends, do they, Dad?" Like Peter Pan, Jason was so immersed at that time in the joy of his social friendships, that he ended up questioning the intrinsic value of growing up at all.

Yet in business, it's true: We so often draw the line on emotional expression and friendship that we fail to be open to learning about the rich resources all around us whether we choose friendship there or not. This is an interesting test, however. How many new friends have you made lately? If you're a true hunter, the answer will include names of quite a few.

Forming new bonds means we are willing to open up and reveal ourselves to the opportunities and potential demands of new relationships. Avid hunters generally have close relationships with their clients, allowing this to evolve naturally.

The best-kept secret to expanding your sandbox, that is, magnifying your assets without enlarging your liabilities too, is to always be on the lookout for the gifts you might find in other people. By focusing on excellence and recognizing it in people with whom you associate, you will find that your network naturally grows in scope and quality, and your range of connectivity and your breadth of perspective grows in turn as well.

BE A TALENT HUNTER

Become a hunter of the talents of others and you will receive two very large gifts. First, you will develop a heightened awareness of opportunities, and, second, you will tap into an enormous wellspring of positive energy. When we keenly observe, identify, and acknowledge others for their skills, individuals open up like bright skies. Most people believe, quite correctly, that they have many underutilized, and certainly unrecognized, talents. By pinpointing, affirming, and nurturing the talents in others, you become a catalyst for creative collaboration and you become a magnet for enviable opportunities.

Once you set this dynamic in motion, you will begin connecting with people around common interests who will become interested in your projects. You will recognize the various ways people want and can be of special assistance to you. Their motivations and goals soon become so evident to you that your helping them becomes instinctive, sensible, and easy to carry out. You'll also more readily envision and share valuable connections and ideas for others.

Can you articulate the real gifts that people in your immediate workspace have to offer? Some of your colleagues are great project managers, some terrific time managers, some excellent relationship managers, and others great coaches, salespeople, number crunchers, or computer wizards. Try acknowledging them, in a most casual or natural way, for their talents, say, at lunch or in a side conversation. Ask a few of them for their advice on something. Try this little exercise with those who work around you and observe what happens. You'll soon see a new form of interaction grow, one that may prove more valuable to both of you than you ever previously thought possible.

LEVERAGING ORGANIZATIONS, ASSOCIATIONS AND AFFINITY GROUPS

More collaboration means greater leverage, which means faster advancement to your end result. Speed is the ultimate currency when it comes to courting the marketplace. You will often move projects or goals along faster if you utilize what's right under your nose, i.e., resources and allies available to you through groups of like-minded or industry-relevant professionals.

EXAMPLE: During a period of recession in the early nineties, when many banks on the East Coast had begun to slow down their high technology lending activities, Silicon Valley Bank decided to enter the Boston market. Tapping Allyn C. Woodward, former high-tech financier with the Bank of New England, as the new market top executive, it opened Silicon Valley Bank East (SVBE) and sent Allyn out to hunt.

Woodward had a great deal of experience to bring to this new arrangement. He'd built strong relationships in the Boston high-tech community over many years, and not only did he know all the top players in the area personally, he also knew where they gathered. By renewing acquaintances and attending, speaking, and participating in area professional associations, he quickly generated a buzz that Silicon Valley Bank East was not only open, but also eager to do business. By the time SVBE's competition awoke from their recessionary slumbers, Woodward had locked up many of the best opportunities that Boston's hi-tech beltway had to offer, firmly establishing Silicon Valley Bank as a major player on both coasts.

Of course, you'll also gain from associations if you actually get involved in them rather than simply join. Professional associations are a terrific way to leverage your relationships because they tend to generate collaborative environments that reward connections and loyalty. Since your network can diminish through entropy, relocations, retirements, and natural attrition, participation in groups delivers much-needed fresh contacts to you on a regular basis.

Other benefits you will accrue include:

- ▲ Professional development
- ▲ Enhanced visibility
- ▲ Market intelligence
- ▲ New learning
- ▲ Stimulation from your new relationships
- ▲ Concentrations of business prospects without their staffs or gatekeepers in the way to keep you apart

To locate names of relevant associations, ask your colleagues, your customers, and your network. Check also **www.asae.com** (the Association of Association Executives) or seek out *The Encyclopedia of Associations* in your library, the *National Trade and Professional*

Associations Yearbook (also in your library), local business journal calendars and business sections of newspapers, and, locally, the Yellow Pages.

BUILD YOUR NIFTY FIFTY

It's all well and good to talk about principles, benefits and results of utilizing PowerSkills, as we've been doing, but there comes a point where you need a framework to help you do it. All throughout the rest of this book, I will attempt to guide you through the creation of this framework.

To start off, the fundamental structure of the entire system will be your "Nifty Fifty" (your 50 key professional contacts). Because you can't possibly cultivate *all* the people you meet in your life, you've got to pick and choose which relationships you'll invest your energy in. These fifty individuals will form the core of your most strategic relationships, your very important relationships, and you will profile them and deepen them and keep them working on your behalf and you on theirs. This doesn't mean that you don't apply these skills to the rest of your relationships but gets you thinking more strategically.

Why fifty? Well, most of us tend to be in contact, whether a little or a lot, on a first-name basis with about 250 people, generally. By injecting Pareto's principle into the process, that is, 80 percent of our bottom-line results in any given area will tend to be derived from 20 percent of the resources available, fifty translates into the most realistic and potent number to get us started.

That may seem like a lot of relationships to manage until you do the math.

Let's say you work fifty weeks per year and had meaningful contact with each of your Nifty Fifty five times per year. At five business days per week, this works out to one Nifty Fifty contact per weekday. With a little discipline, such an objective is very achievable. One a day. Sound familiar? Regular value added communications with your Nifty Fifty can make the difference between an ordinary or magnificent professional life.

To select your Nifty Fifty, think about the people you know and make a list of those who fit most or all of the following criteria of each individual:

▲ shares your core values.

▲ is someone you feel you could build a significant business relationship with.

▲ has great relationships and experiences with others who might also be valuable to you.

▲ has a position or influence in your organization or market space that's important to you.

▲ has goals that are synergistic with your own.

▲ could be one of tomorrow's stars.

▲ is capable of inspiring you and generating positive motivation.

Once you've brainstormed this list of people who meet your criteria, add such categorical information as professional title, company/employer, line of business, customer. You'll also want to record their groupings (be sure to make groupings that suit you, e.g., general managers, buying influencers, consultants, colleagues, recruiters, bankers). Capture any action items as next steps that you should be taking with this person.

▶ **EXHIBIT 5.1 Basic Profile**

Name:	Joan Grady
Title:	VP Information Services
Company:	Widener Hospital
Category:	Technical Operations
Customer?	Yes
Groupings:	Mid-market Health Care Executive; Board member, Arts and theatre
Action Needed:	Expand the current business relationship

Look at Exhibit 5.1, which demonstrates a Nifty Fifty grid for Joan Grady. Notice how we're capturing basic information so that we can than move on to "calibrate" and "profile". First, we need to ask ourselves a few important questions. Answers to these questions will help us rate the importance of each contact and the urgency with which we need to take appropriate actions with them.

▲ Have I spent sufficient time with this VIR over the past six months? To answer this question, I must calibrate my relationship.

▲ What else should I know about Joan? Profiling my contacts will help me know more and build depth.

▲ How valuable are my groupings? Once I've grouped all my contacts by their key interests and activities, I'll know how Joan's groupings fit into my Nifty Fifty and how value can be created.

▲ What actions will help to grow or add value to this VIR? Recording my key actions whenever I deliver my added value helps me evaluate these actions.

▲ What can I do to become a Nifty Fifty contact for Joan? Understanding and providing my added value to her can help here.

▲ What's the best way to stay in touch with Joan? Choosing appropriately from a range of communication options should be considered.

▲ How can I expand the range of my contacts? When I leverage key organizations, associations and affinity groups, expansion will happen.

▲ How can I manage all of this information and activity? A periodic process review of all my VIRs will help me to manage this abundant interaction. Later in Chapter 10 we will discuss easy-to-use technology.

If your goal is to become fully proficient in building, growing, and maintaining your Nifty Fifty, you will want to use this list as a part of a comprehensive process for managing your resource network and keeping it relevant.

CALIBRATE YOUR NIFTY FIFTY

To *calibrate* means to check, adjust, or determine by comparison with a standard. Your list needs to be calibrated because otherwise you won't know the relative importance of each contact and therefore won't know which contacts should be on your Nifty Fifty. I developed this relationship planning technique (the Archer Relationship Management Index®) at Archer Development for our Corporate Education Programs.

The Archer Relationship Index®, is a strategic tool for calibrating your professional network and prioritizing your relationships according to four dimensions: depth, relevance, position, and influence. By scoring each of these dimensions on a five-point scale, you can quickly derive a raw score for each relationship and gain valuable insight as to where minimum effort realizes maximum results. The very act of making these assessments forces you to re-evaluate your assumptions about existing relationships, evolving roles, potential opportunities, and immediate actions that can be mutually beneficial. Evaluating your web of relationships in this way helps you to measure your progress in building relationships in terms of quality, quantity, and level.

Using the Archer Relationship Index®, together with the Nifty Fifty analysis allows management teams to quickly assess their relationship assets and gaps, to achieve new initiatives. Let's look at Exhibit 5.2 to see how the index works.

► EXHIBIT 5.2 Archer Relationship Index®

POINTS	DEPTH	RELEVANCE	POSITION	INFLUENCE
1	Rapport	Opportunistic	Contact	Resource
2	Respect	Specialty	Gatekeeper	Expert
3	Disclosure	Emergent	Guide	Rising Star
4	Commitment	Valued	Key Influencer	Opinion Leader/Sage
5	Partnership	Critical	Decision-Maker	Industry Leader

▶ Archer Relationship Index® – DEFINITIONS

DEPTH The depth dimension ranks the developed status of your personal and professional relationship with the contact person.

RAPPORT (1 POINT)

▶ Initial reaction is positive.
▶ Communication is comfortable.
▶ Next steps are possible.

RESPECT (2 POINTS)

▶ The contact respects you as a unique individual.
▶ The contact understands your added value and professional skills.
▶ The contact would consider doing business with you.

DISCLOSURE (3 POINTS)

▶ The relationship has evolved to mutual sharing of professional and perhaps personal confidences and expectations.
▶ The relationship can now grow quickly to the next level.

COMMITMENT (4 POINTS)

▶ The relationship is characterized by both parties making and keeping professional commitments.
▶ Contracting is predictable.

PARTNERSHIP (5 POINTS)

▶ The relationship has reached the highest level of professional relationship, trust and collaboration.
▶ The relationship has been tested with constructive confrontations.
▶ Each person shows an interest in the other person's success.

▶ **Archer Relationship Index® – DEFINITIONS**

RELEVANCE The relevance dimension records your assessment of the strategic value that the contact's organization has to your organization.

OPPORTUNISTIC (1 POINT)
▶ The relationship is unexplored, so opportunities and potential fit for the contact's company are unclear.
▶ The relationship may yield a one-time opportunity.

SPECIALTY (2 POINTS)
▶ This is a customer or supplier relationship in a specialty area.
▶ The business relationship currently exploits a narrow but productive niche.

EMERGENT (3 POINTS)
▶ The relationship has apparent long-term potential; too early to predict the success of the partnership or the technical success or marketability of the concept.
▶ The relationship now involves committing significant resources.

VALUED (4 POINTS)
▶ It is important to maintain and broaden the relationship.
▶ You have developed a mature relationship with this organization.
▶ The contact and organization is a good reference.
▶ The relationship is approaching the point of advocacy.

CRITICAL (5 POINTS)
▶ The mission is of critical strategic importance to your company and its core business.
▶ It is important to expend every effort to sustain, grow, and protect the relationship.
▶ Mutual advocacy and long-term planning exist.

Archer Relationship Index® – DEFINITIONS

POSITION   The position dimension ranks the level of power and influence of the contact person's position in his or her organization relative to the contact's ability or interest in your project or critical issues.

CONTACT (1 POINT)

▶ The individual is a basic contact for you within the organization; basic rapport.

▶ This individual is a former colleague or acquaintance who is new to the organization; not yet established power or influence.

GATEKEEPER (2 POINTS)

▶ This contact person screens or reviews your product/service offerings.

▶ This contact person has some influence to control outcomes or access to influences or decision-makers.

▶ This contact person is not the final decision-maker.

GUIDE (3 POINTS)

▶ The contact is a proponent of your project.

▶ He or she will guide you towards meeting your objectives as you deal with that organization.

▶ The contact has credibility within his or her own organization.

▶ The contact person has no direct authority over your project.

KEY INFLUENCER (4 POINTS)

▶ This individual is actively involved in your project.

▶ This individual has a strong influence position.

▶ This individual has some project-related authority.

DECISION-MAKER (5 POINTS)

▶ This person has authority, influence, responsibility, and budget resources to accept or implement your ideas, products or services.

▶ Archer Relationship Index® – DEFINITIONS

INFLUENCE The influence dimension records your estimate of the power and influence level of the contact person beyond their company to your marketplace.

RESOURCE (1 POINT)

▶ This relationship is with a knowledgeable professional, consultant, or manager with a low-profile in your industry.

▶ This relationship can help in accessing people or information.

EXPERT (2 POINTS)

▶ The contact person is extremely knowledgeable in the specific area of your industry or endeavor.

▶ The contact person has influence when the subject matter expertise is brought to bear on a decision.

RISING STAR (3 POINTS)

▶ The individual is an emerging leader, manager, or established mid-level professional with growing credibility in the industry.

▶ The individual has a broader scope of knowledge and contacts than the expert.

OPINION LEADER/SAGE (4 POINTS)

▶ This person has a significant credibility and long-term experience in the industry. *Examples*: highly regarded sales executive, retired CEO who sits on boards, advisor or top-notch consultant having significant influence but no specific position authority.

INDUSTRY LEADER (5 POINTS)

▶ This person is a recognized mover and shaker in the industry.

▶ This person is possibly a CEO, lead investor, senior editor or author.

▶ This person's endorsement carries the highest credibility.

Calibration using the Archer Relationship Index®

Now let's calibrate Joan Grady with respect to the four dimensions of Depth, Relevance, Position, and Influence.

1. **DEPTH: RESPECT (LEVEL 2).** You have only recently met Joan through a mutual colleague who highly respects the work you do and her department recently used your services on a small project. She understands your added value and might consider doing business with you again in the near future and for now is willing to provide some useful information. You've just picked up on the fact that Joan is active in the arts and theatre like your self and some of your colleagues. You recognize that it's time to get to know Joan and her needs better or all your future communications could be re-routed to her staff.

2. **RELEVANCE: EMERGENT (LEVEL 3).** The initial project was successful and there's long-term potential with Joan's organization but without more information, it's too early to predict the possible scope of work. She's shown a willingness to commit some significant time to help out with a management briefing and make some additional introductions outside the hospital. You know that the capabilities of your firm could be a match for the needs of a hospital of this size.

3. **POSITION: DECISION-MAKER (LEVEL 5).** Joan is in a very strong position at the hospital. You want to discuss with her your plans for serving Widener Hospital on new fronts. You want to get her authorization directly for some initiatives and, for other initiatives, enlist her strong influence on other decision-makers.

4. **INFLUENCE: OPINION LEADER (LEVEL 4).** Joan is a recognized name in her industry. Her endorsement carries some credibility.

With your contacts and enthusiasm for the quality of her operation, she could become an industry leader that is asked to sit on more boards.

Joan's score for DRPI (Depth, Relevance, Position, Influence) is 2 + 3 + 5 + 4 = 14. Fourteen of twenty possible points make Joan a key player. The action items now become more focused with the analysis of the DRPI (See Exhibit 5.3).

▶ **EXHIBIT 5.3 Calibrated Profile**

Name:	Joan Grady
Title:	VP Information Services
Company:	Widener Hospital
Category:	Technical Operations
Customer:	Yes
Groupings:	Mid-market Health Care Executive; Board member, Arts and theatre
Depth:	*Respect – 2 points*
Relevance:	*Emergent – 3 points*
Position:	*Decision-Maker – 5 points*
Influence:	*Opinion Leader – 4 points*
Actions:	▶ Expand the current business relationship.
	▶ Improve the depth of the relationship–face time and profiling.
	▶ Conduct a needs assessment at the hospital to scope a larger long term project.
	▶ Recognize Joan as a decision-maker and prepare an analysis for her.
	▶ Assist Joan in furthering her interests in public speaking and board of director assignments.
	▶ Invite her Management team to a local theatre event.

EXERCISE:

Calibrate your entire Nifty Fifty list by evaluating each contact in light of the four dimensions: *depth* (quality and status of your relationship), *relevance* (strategic organizational fit with your organization's needs), *position* (the contact's rank and power within their company), *influence* (the contact's influence outside his or her firm but within your marketplace).

After calibrating your list, revise your action items based upon a clearer view of each relative ranking. Consider doing this exercise quarterly, adding and pruning your Nifty Fifty list and following through on your written action items as you build toward a stronger base with a second Nifty Fifty behind it!

When completed, each Nifty Fifty list can score a maximum of 1000 possible points (maximum of 5 points on 4 scales multiplied by 50). Since not all key contacts need be at the partnership level, a score in the 700s would be indicative of an advanced PowerSkills practitioner with a formidable asset. This is the only known technique to quantitatively and qualitatively assess and prioritize a VIP (or VIR) database and drive specific campaigns for a management, engineering, sales, marketing, or customer service team. Conducting this exercise dramatically expands your capacity to manage strategic relationships strategically.

PROFILE YOUR VIRS

Having calibrated your very important relationships (VIRs), you next will want to "profile" them. This means determining what information you need from them (planning), beginning to build relationships with each contact through active listening and coaching skills, creating a relationship development strategy that is unique to each individual or group, and building a stay-in-touch program. We will discuss who to profile in more detail in later

---

▶ **EXHIBIT 5.4   Profile Checklist**

Main Contact Record		Company Information	Activity, History and Account Information
Last update, date, by	Cell phone	Company description	Customer ID #
Title	Pager	Mission statement	Billing address
First Name	Assistant name, info	# employees	Shipping address
Last Name	Address 2	Distribution channels	Date of 1st purchase
Nick name	Address 3	Divisions	Dates of purchases
Company	Groups assigned	Products	Items purchased
Address 1 (Company)	Previous employment 1	Services	Distribution channel
Company	Title	Top customers	Purchase amounts
Division	Company	Major suppliers	Average order size
Suite	Division	Board members	How purchase
Street	Years	Business partners	was made
City	Previous employment 2	Strategy	Source of business
State	Education 1	Competitors	Competitor
Zip	Degree	Competitive threats	information
Tele Main	School	Key decision makers	Notes
Extension	Year	Intelligence	
Tele Direct	Education 2	requirements	
Voice Mail	Education 3	Organization	
Email	Notes	Notes	
Internet/URL			

Analysis & Plan	Personal Information		Significant Networks
RFM:	Home town	Favorite meals,	Alumni clubs
- Recency	School activities	entertain	Social clubs
- Frequency	Family information	Outside interests	Sports clubs
- Monetary Analysis	Spouse name	Career obj. short term	Directorships
Archer Index®	Spouse education	Career obj. long term	Associations
Relationship Action	Spouse occupation	Investments	Memberships
Plan	Children's names, ages	Advisors	Volunteer
Dialogue mix	Personality type	Descriptive adjectives	organizations
Notes	Automobile	Reading habits	Notes
	Medical history	Social concerns	
		Business philosophy	
		Notes	

chapters, but one important tool you can use is a *profiling checklist* like the one in Exhibit 5.4. It is adapted from The Archer Profile Checklist, which is used by companies to develop their field names for customer relationship management databases.

This checklist will help you to enter information about your very important relationships and to also be aware of the questions to keep in mind as you compile the profile data. The checklist will also allow you to develop closer relationships through conversations with your VIRs. The fact that you are taking an interest by asking some questions relating to these items will bring you closer to the individual. In spite of what they might say, the most interesting topic for people is themselves! Your style of asking and profiling should be natural and informal and may even take place over a period of time. Few of your Nifty Fifty will ever be profiled to the full extent of this checklist, but having these field names makes it easy to capture the information, identify the gaps, enter and conduct searches from a database, and tailor your communications and plan events for people with common interests.

EXERCISE:

Refer to the Profile Checklist and begin to profile several members of your Nifty Fifty list. With your new insight, you will see that your DRPI assessments and your action items will change accordingly.

Once you've completed creating, calibrating and profiling your Nifty Fifty list, you'll be organized to hunt and collaborate with great effectiveness especially when integrated with the next PowerSkill, coaching. Your calibration and profiling of your contacts will help you understand what action items you should undertake toward building a vibrant Nifty Fifty list and in what priority. Among the action items you will often want to prioritize for any and all of your VIRs should be a readiness to provide coaching. If you're always prepared to give to another, you'll strengthen the willingness of others to give to you. Call it karma or call it business common sense—it works.

PowerSkills should not be confused with what people have for years been referring to as networking. The emphasis here is on building key relationships to create specific value, not just compiling random contacts. Sure, networking is a piece of it—meeting people in various ways and getting their contact information—but it is rudimentary. Networking is really a part of hunting, and is part of one PowerSkill only. Only by developing *all* of the PowerSkills can we truly optimize those relationship assets that traditional networking might initiate.

Many sales VPs don't believe people can be taught to hunt, so they don't try. This is a mistake. As I said earlier in this chapter, hunters generally are made, not born. I also pointed out that many business leaders take their PowerSkills for granted, not realizing that passing them on to others, (training their people), represents the only truly effective way to get departments and organizations operating at the highest levels. Yet while many great business leaders have developed superb PowerSkills themselves, they haven't a clue how to teach others to do the same.

From my observations, most professionals in the workplace can learn PowerSkills and take on higher-level capacities in their jobs. If you're a solid PowerSkill performer now but haven't communicated how to effectively manage the key relationships of your business to your people, move on to the next chapter and learn about PowerSkill #3, coaching.

CHAPTER KEY POINTS

▲ Like their counterparts in the scientific and explorer realms, business hunters are seekers of value, possibilities, excitement, and new opportunities.

▲ From executives to college professors to research librarians to art collectors, upon investigation, you will find that the most successful in each category will be its hunters.

▲ Hunting, no matter how strongly affected by innate talent or cultural conditioning, can be learned.

▲ Successful hunters have a search methodology.

▲ Hunters consistently expand their spheres of influence over time.

▲ Become a hunter of the talents of others and you will spark productive and creative collaborations.

▲ Your calibration and profiling of contacts helps you understand what action items to undertake and help you build and leverage a vibrant Nifty Fifty.

▲ More collaboration means greater leverage, meaning faster advancement to your end result.

QUESTIONS FOR YOUR POWERSKILLS JOURNAL

▲ Have you built fifty top-level business relationships that will help you achieve your objectives?

▲ What is the composition and level of the people on your list?

▲ Can they provide you with the business intelligence and introductions that you need?

▲ Are you spending your professional time with the right people?

▲ Do you have easy access to these influencers and decision-makers?

▲ Are they invested in your success?

▲ What value have you produced for these key relationships over the past year?

▲ Have you profiled their interests, goals, and needs to understand how you can create some value for them?

PRACTICE TIPS

▲ Put together the best list of strategic relationships you now have and calibrate using the Archer Relationship Index. Are you batting over 400? 600? What is important is that you begin with what you have, even if it is five key relationships.

▲ As you go through the analysis, write out your action items and follow-through.

▲ Profile a few of these top people artfully over the next few weeks. Try to identify the talents they are most proud of. Recognize them for it in some follow up. Find ways to collaborate that benefit you both.

▲ Organize your list into groups (constituencies)—clients, prospects, service providers, technical resources, and so on.

▲ Identify a key organization or association that your most important constituency participates in, and then get involved. Expand your relationships in that grouping by providing some unique value.

RESOURCES

Click on **www.powerskills.com/hunting** for readings, links, and resources to develop this skill.

Networking with the Affluent and Their Advisors by Dr. Thomas J. Stanley. Burr Ridge, IL: Irwin Professional Publishing, 1993. ISBN 1-55623-891-6

Networking Smart: How to Build Relationships for Personal and Organizational Success by Wayne E. Baker. New York: McGraw-Hill Inc., 1994. ISBN 0-07-005092-9

Selling to the Top by David A. Peoples. New York: John Wiley & Sons, Inc., 1993. ISBN 0-471-58104-6

Solution Selling: Creating Buyers in Difficult Selling Markets by Michael T. Bosworth. Burr Ridge, IL: Irwin Professional Publishing, 1995. ISBN 0-7863-0315-8

The WarRoom: Guide to Competitive Intelligence by Steven M. Shaker and Mark P. Gembicki. New York: McGraw-Hill, 1999. ISBN 0-07-058057-X

CHAPTER 6

POWERSKILL #3: COACHING

"You aren't really listening unless you are willing to be changed by what you hear."

—Redford Williams, M.D.

When the United States Women's World Soccer Team captivated the hearts of its nation in the summer of 1999 by defeating all comers, culminating in a dramatic grand finale against China in the Rose Bowl before 100,000 screaming fans, it triumphed for women athletes the world over, for soccer in America, and for the possibilities one can expect from brilliant coaching. The team had come a long way since suffering a heartbreaking loss to Norway four years earlier in Sweden. As the ecstatic Norwegians danced a conga line around the field after the game officially ended, everyone connected with the U.S. team vowed to never let it happen again.

It was the job of Head Coach Tony DiCicco to take the ball from there. A former coach of many men's soccer teams, DiCicco rightly judged that this time his coaching methods demanded more. While sports coaching traditionally has often focused on yelling, exhorting, pointing out weaknesses, and instilling fear and urgency, DiCicco this time considered reversing such methods.

"Men can absorb tough criticism because they don't really believe it anyway," he explained to *Newsweek* after the World's Cup victory. "Women believe it and take it to heart. So I tried to coach positive."

Coaching positive meant showing more sensitivity for his individual performers. Postgame videos, for example, never showed goof-ups or embarrassments, even the goal the United States had inadvertently scored for Germany in '95. Instead, players reviewed moves and maneuvers that worked—high points that reminded them how good they could be and how they should continue to act and react in order to win.

The results speak for themselves, and one wonders why male athletes wouldn't respond just as positively to the same techniques. Whether in sports or business or just life in general, positive beats negative, and paying real attention to a person beats ignoring or browbeating.

To develop from "star" performer or "boss" to "coach" is difficult for many professionals to understand, embrace, or implement. More than simply a matter of having patience, coaching is a developed PowerSkill that engages others in changing their own behaviors for best results. While being a leader and being a coach can at first glance appear distinctly different activities, the qualities of great leaders and great coaches are nearly identical.

The third PowerSkill, coaching, actually holds the key to operating effective relationship networks. We've already examined how important it is to manage your web of strategic relationships inside and outside your company. A coaching mindset, in addition, introduces empathy, respect and collaboration to your human network. Create an atmosphere of "Coach and Be Coached" and you will unlock the creative potential of your organization and reduce "FUD"—fear, uncertainty, and doubt. These three corrosive buddies show up all too frequently in today's low-trust workplaces.

Coaching is a means of deepening your business relationships. You don't have to enter into a formal coaching relationship to coach and be coached. By asking open-ended questions about all kinds of matters, that is, by just being curious (but with a purpose), you can continue the profiling process and add value to your VIR's business life and to your own.

PROFILING INITIATES COACHING-LIKE RELATIONSHIPS

When you are establishing a new relationship think about a casual interview process that may extend over time. Begin the process by asking about (and recording) basic contact information such as phone, fax, and email, and basic company information like mission statement, top customers, products, Board members, and so on. If the person is a customer, you want to also capture such activity and history items as dates of purchases, purchase amounts, competitor information. Other categories will also deepen your relationship with this person including:

your "analysis-and-relationship plan" for this contact (recency and frequency of purchases, your own projection of this contact's value to you and yours to her), "personal information" (spouses' occupation, hometown, career objectives, reading habits), and "significant networks" (alumni clubs, directorships, professional associations).

With sincere interest, begin the deepening process by asking open-ended questions, especially about the person's views on certain topics. Examples: What got you started in this business? Tell me about your professional relationships? What's your philosophy of doing business in this industry? What skills are you most known for?

Again, it is an ongoing atmosphere you want to create between yourself and a contact. I have often said, "Make friends of your clients and turn your business friends into coaches." By starting the process in the very beginning, you make clearer to both parties how your relationship can serve you both.

For example, coaching is the best way to create learning relationships all around you, and we all know that learning faster than the competition is what will give any organization a powerful edge today. To engage in coaching is to dialogue with customers, suppliers, and business partners and to build bonds that last, creating value beyond the expected all the way to the unanticipated. This provides a business friendship "currency" offering many dividends.

Though coaching is a must for managers needing to help subordinates problem solve, it can also impact relationships far beyond the company and create new value. Many excellent books and articles and leading thinkers extol the virtues of coaching in business today, yet from what I've seen, most managers and business leaders do actual coaching only rarely. That's why much of this chapter will be devoted to exploring the key principles of coaching, including how to develop coaching skills, what prevents most leaders from excelling at coaching, and how to apply this PowerSkill in the broadest context.

THE HUMAN TOUCH

Coaching is a relationship-builder. It also reinforces your desired positioning. Let's say that your goal is to be perceived as a trusted advisor to your clients and industry leaders. Your attractiveness as a coach will be paramount to achieving this goal. In fact, you know you have really developed this skill when your Nifty Fifty relationships view and utilize you as a coaching resource. Unfortunately, few MBA or business courses include this learning activity in their curriculums.

Coaching humanizes business relationships, putting the human touch back into business. Not only will coaching make a "value deposit" into your one-to-one relationships with key clients and colleagues but you will also begin recognizing the transformative power of coaching both teams and organizations. Influencing large groups is not just the province of a "bully pulpit" from a high position—great coaches can have a large-scale impact too!

To evolve from star performer to leader to coach takes resolve. Many people would simply rather exhort others to "just do it," "take action," and get people "moving." Yet the most skillful leaders have learned to coach as a way of being—it's an automatic component of their set of PowerSkills. In an environment where we all need to be effective at managing relationships that may be dispersed all over the globe, coaching skills allow us to create close but low-maintenance relationships. Skilled coaching infuses greater self-reliance in others while, on the flip side, ineffectual coaching, like poor parenting, often fosters dependency.

To be effective as a coach, each of us must commit ourselves to genuine self-development, exemplifying the characteristics that attract people to each other: empathy, respect, integrity, an open mind, humility, straight talk, the ability to ask insightful questions, and a drive for excellence. This sets a standard for ourselves that propels us in our enabling of profound possibilities in others. Though coaching methods and techniques abound, good coaching is in fact largely a matter of self-discipline and self-mastery. When seen as a calling it not only improves our ability to focus keenly on others but also provides a golden opportunity to better know ourselves.

THE COACHING MOMENT

Coaching moments can occur at any time (spontaneous or planned), anywhere, or in any way (formal or informal). As indicated earlier, they can occur with subordinates, co-workers, your VIRs, or any trust-based relationships. The "shape" of a coaching moment is shown in Exhibit 6.1. The characteristics of collaborative coaching conversations are determined by: (a) a signal to get started, (b) a clearly agreed-upon, up-front coaching goal that really gets the shaping process moving, (c) a conversation flow that expands information initially, then focuses the use of it to formulate courses of action, and (d) a "performance agreement" of what the coachee will do and when. Contained within this model is a particularly good acronym outlined in the book *The Tao of Coaching* by Max Landsberg—"G.R.O.W.," that is, Goal, Reality, Options, and Wrap-up. The idea of G.R.O.W. is described by Landsberg as follows:

First explore the goal to be accomplished, then debate and discuss *reality* versus perception, next review *options and alternatives,* finally *wrap up* your coaching session with an agreed-upon action item or next step. It's a simple, sequential process that moves smoothly from idea to implementation and provides the proper flow for effective coaching moments.

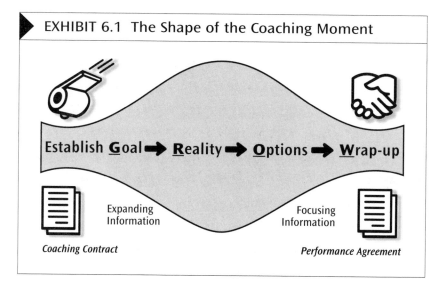

EXHIBIT 6.1 The Shape of the Coaching Moment

Establish **G**oal ➡ **R**eality ➡ **O**ptions ➡ **W**rap-up

Expanding Information

Focusing Information

Coaching Contract

Performance Agreement

COACHING TYPES

Because coaching can have very different goals, there are three primary types of coaching. Some coaching for example will be aimed at problem solving. Another reason to coach will be to improve a direct report's performance. Still another coaching goal would be to assist another's process of personal transformation. In this section, we explore all three, taking into account the challenges and best practices of each type.

Coaching to Solve Problems

The challenge here is the same as with all coaching—get the coachee to understand relevant facts, define the problem correctly, explore options, gain confidence, and take responsibility for a designated correct action. The distinguishing characteristic of this coaching type is the level of personal change required of the coachee. Coaching to solve problems is an important if relatively fundamental coaching skill, involving clarifying, asking, listening, communicating respect, reflecting and possibly sharing similar life experiences in order to help the coachee to move from insight to action (or choice). It represents essentially a nurturing activity that will take place in those situations when on-the-spot coaching is requested or needed.

Often, an individual will seek your help to make a particularly difficult decision among several complex choices. The person may be seeing the choices as overwhelming because of being pulled in different emotional directions by some of the variables. Worse, the information to make an easy decision may not be available. In this situation a useful coaching tool is to build a decision matrix with the coachee. The following example represents a common situation in which an individual is trying to make a deeply personal choice of work assignments but the technique can be used for any decisions in which analysis of many variables is required.

EXAMPLE: Suppose a long-term client of yours, in this case a senior executive, confides in you about a coming reorganization in which three possible career choices will be available for her. Each, she explains, carries with it both positives and negatives. After much careful listening and probing, you believe you have sorted out the knowns from the unknowns, in the process observing great amounts of emotion and ambivalence associated with each choice. You introduce the idea of doing a decision matrix to prioritize variables, weights, and ratings for each choice.

The completed decision matrix, Exhibit 6.2, demonstrates the variables, weighting, and rating for each choice that was identified in the coaching session.

▶ EXHIBIT 6.2 The Decision Matrix

Variables Weighted 1-10	COURSES OF ACTION		
	Choice A Current Job	Choice B Lateral Move	Choice C New Opportunity
Family Impact (8)	Excellent (16)	Excellent (16)	Poor ? (-8)
The Boss (7)	Excellent (14)	Good (7)	Good ? (7)
New Learning (7)	Fair (0)	Good (7)	Excellent (14)
Compensation (6)	Fair (0)	Fair (0)	Excellent (12)
Travel Requirements (4)	Excellent (8)	Good (4)	Fair (0)
Local Interests (3)	Excellent (6)	Excellent (6)	Grim (-6)
Resume Builder (6)	Fair (0)	Good (6)	Excellent (12)
Network (5)	Fair (0)	Good (5)	Excellent (10)
TOTALS:	44	51	41
KEY: Excellent = 2, Good = 1, Fair = 0, Poor = –1, Grim = –2			

COURSES OF ACTION—In this example, Choice A is to to continue working for the same boss. The client likes and has loyalty to this boss; there is a promise of an appealing new assignment in six months. Choice B is to transfer laterally to another group. The work is very interesting, with the opportunity to learn some new skills right away and make some new connections that will be useful to the next career step. Choice C is an exceptional and exciting new opportunity outside the company in a bigger job with more pay but involves a relocation.

VARIABLES—In this case, eight variables were selected with the coach that would have an effect on the choice. Tradeoffs between loyalty to the boss, compensation, new learning, impact on the family, continuing local community activities, relocation, amount of travel required, career development and improving the influence network in the industry are all considered and weighted on a scale of 110.

SCORING—Once the choices are rated, the scores are tallied by multiplying the weights times the numerical ratings. Since a Fair rating is a neutral response, it has a zero value. Question marks are placed beside ratings that are based upon limited information that may need to be tested or collected before the matrix can really be completed. If the highest score does not resonate emotionally with the coachee as the best choice then it is likely that there is a missing variable, incorrect assumptions around the weightings, or that there is a lack of information in key cells of the matrix. Further discussion would be needed to complete the process. In this case, the client decided that the best risk/reward choice was to take choice B, a Idevelopment assignment with the same company. The important point is that the process helped to clarify the tradeoffs and steps required to make the best informed decision.

Coaching to Improve Performance

Coaching for improved performance goes beyond helping others to solve problems or make better decisions. This type of coaching influences the leverage points for real behavioral change, i.e., those factors that contribute to true transformation. To be effective here requires that a relationship has evolved fully into one of empathy and respect. We are now talking not merely of nurturing and responding but outright influencing another person (with his/her permission) to effect a behavior change that will significantly improve performance. This means more action-oriented, high-risk, initiative behavior on the part of both coach and coachee. It also involves digging deep for root causes and overcoming resistance to change. A level of constructive confrontation of issues, behaviors, and consequences may also be required. The issue for most professionals is: How to do this without raising defenses or projecting onto the situation your own needs?

And this is precisely what stops most managers dead in their tracks, the fear that they don't know when they are "crossing a line" while offering feedback designed to motivate another to act in the best way possible. One rule of thumb is to keep the conversation focused on shared objectives, providing feedback on specific performance and behaviors while getting the coachee, without feeling threatened, to explore his own possible "blocks" to improve. We are not trying here to serve up theories of psychological antecedents for behaviors—we'll leave that to licensed psychotherapists. Nonetheless, some history of giving quality feedback on both desired and unsatisfactory performance will build a foundation to address more difficult issues within a business context.

Some appropriate use of self-disclosure by the coach, by sharing common experiences in overcoming obstacles, or by relating anecdotal examples, can also be used to make it easier for the coachee to open up, at a deeper level, that is, get to the heart of a matter. Before a coach can effectively move to a confrontation successfully, the base of trust and faith in the spirit of the message must be established. When a coach opens herself up, the coachee is provided a model to do the same.

EXAMPLE: Let's say a VP of Marketing we'll call Rick has been trying for some time to raise a "sense of urgency" in Tom, one of his subordinates. A talented marketing manager, promoted several years ago from engineering, Tom works long hours, is team-oriented, well-liked, and willing to take on a lot of tasks. His problem, as Rick sees it: Tom's projects are usually late and he often has trouble seeing the larger context for the work he is assigned. People who work for Tom frequently wait for him to make his decisions, often going into "neutral" at such times, then resenting last-minute rush jobs he creates. When he does come through, however, the quality of his completed staff work is impeccable.

As Tom's manager, Rick feels completely buffaloed by this paradox of talent and inefficiency. Some days he wonders if Tom is really cut out for senior management at all. On such days, Rick further realizes that "raising a sense of urgency" in Tom is only the tip of the iceberg: time management, prioritizing, delegating, an overly internal focus, "seeing the big picture"—all are pieces of Tom's particular performance puzzle.

As personalities, Tom and Rick are opposites, making it hard for Rick to identify with Tom's deficiencies. So used to naturally balancing process with the need for bottom-line results, Rick's admonitions to Tom to "just do it" haven't been helping one bit. He finally realizes that, while he has spent lots of time with Tom trying to problem-solve his lack of business results, he has not provided Tom even five minutes of performance-improvement coaching over the course of six months. His feedback has mostly consisted of emotional expressions of exasperation that things are not moving more quickly and suggestions for steps Tom can take to turn his behavior around. It is time, Rick tells himself, to change his approach.

He sits down with Tom, determined to focus on the dancer and the dance. "Tom," he begins, "let's look at the last three projects that you've completed and three others that have been incomplete for months. Tell me about the resources that you are using to complete these projects. What can the company provide to move things along?"

Tom admits he has plenty of resources, there really isn't anything else he needs. "I understand, better than anyone," he says, "that all three of these projects should have been completed by now."

After continued questioning by Rick, using questions designed to probe not blame, Tom begins to share his own frustration with his perfectionist personality. Worrying about how the job will get done, for example, makes it difficult for him to delegate to others. Working so long and hard has even affected his marriage. Tom's willingness to share such personal details opens the whole session up to discussion of the career-limiting aspects of Tom's operating style.

With Tom focusing now on his behaviors, Rick convenes a meeting with the marketing management group that includes Tom. A result of this meeting is that the team comes up with a standard format for project planning and review, and Tom enthusiastically agrees to initiate it with a complete review of his own projects.

The next day, Rick sits in on Tom's presentation and observes how freely Tom expresses how he has been a bottleneck to the group. He then outlines steps he plans to take to get his projects back on track. Along with team suggestions for flowcharts and reports consisting of milestones and deadlines, and Rick's own ideas for customer-feedback sessions and weekly status reports, Tom's situation turns around 180 degrees. His projects begin coming in on time, he delegates assignments more easily, and he even goes to Rick for problem-solving coaching whenever he gets stuck. In addition to Rick's heightened satisfaction of Tom's performance, others in upper management come to view Tom's work positively, and he is considered for a promotion within six months of beginning Rick's performance-improvement coaching.

You can see from this example that Rick was able to generate new behavior from Tom by ending a command-and-control style (born of frustration) and working with Tom in a supportive, though direct, manner. He asked such questions as "What are the barriers to completing this project by the end of the quarter?" and "What things can you do differently to speed up your projects?" He tried to frame questions that invited mutual discussion, not defensiveness. Because of this approach, Tom quickly realized that Rick was indeed committed to his development.

Fortunately for Rick, Tom proved extremely "coachable," that is, open to both feedback and change. In some ways, you may wish that this kind of "adult supervision" wasn't needed but in reality, if you don't employ it, you'll end up spending more time on matters with fewer results. If, like Rick, you fail to pick up the performance improvement ball and instead keep trying to get your subordinates to "just do it," much will be lost in the interim.

Coaching for Personal Transformation

In the previous two coaching types, coaching helped improve performance by dealing with on-the-spot work problems and behaviors and with their consequences. But the last type involves much stronger medicine. Helping a guy like Tom, for example, who tends to get bogged down in details, become a real leader would necessitate getting him out of his comfort zone. It would demand that Tom visualize himself in a totally new context and overcome his early training. He would need to begin seeing himself as a decision-maker rather than as a peacemaker. He would need to focus more on winning than on seeking approval, oriented to the bottom line more than on abstract ideas. Coaching at this level requires a special relationship rare in business. For that reason alone, coaching for personal transformation, unfortunately, is rarely done.

Needed transformations vary from individual to individual. Common ones include:

▲ From fear of failure to a passion to win

▲ From "What's in it for me?" to "How can I help?"

▲ From defensiveness to defenselessness

▲ From controlling behavior to acceptance and responsibility in actions

▲ From competing and comparing with others to discovering one's true identity

▲ From seeking security to seeking excellence

▲ From seeking approval to finding creative expression

▲ From self-destructive to self-renewing behaviors

▲ From sloppy thinking to disciplined learning

EXAMPLE: While at the helm of an executive recruiting firm, my partners and I grew frustrated with the disappointing results we usually obtained whenever we recruited experienced search consultants. Our frustration even extended to efforts to lure a "star performer" from the competition. Often, to our chagrin, we were really snaring the lower performers who were the most recruitable. We gradually learned we had higher standards than most of our competitors so that a new recruit's sloppy work habits, acceptable at other firms, were a liability with us.

One day, I made a bold pronouncement to my partners that my next associate hire was going to be a novice, a real greenhorn, maybe two years out of college and with no experience whatsoever in our industry. "What's more," I proclaimed, "we will develop this untried novice into a top performer!" I simply wanted, I added, to find someone with integrity, good people skills, and real desire. My partners literally laughed at me, calling my idea a waste of time and a certain-to-fail experiment. Most of the people in our organization were MBAs with at least ten years of experience in the business, and since we were focused on the high-technology industry, they all had significant knowledge and experience in that industry as well.

About a month later, I visited a car dealership when looking to buy a new car. While the salesman was busy with another customer, Will, a young factory-service representative whose job it was to visit local dealerships and help improve operations and product knowledge of sales staffs, spent time with me explaining all the new models. Will's enthusiasm for his company's products was contagious, so much so that as he was about to introduce me to one of the "real" salespeople, I said, no, that wouldn't be necessary and bought a car from him on the spot. Will said he loved these cars and he loved the company even though he was only a "leased employee" with no benefits (and long hours and low pay). He didn't receive commissions and he hadn't been given much training. At this point, he confided to me, he wasn't even sure about his future, but he didn't seem to care. He had a wonderful wife, he said, who worked as a dental assistant and the couple had no children.

Since casual interviewing is a habit of mine, I got to know him very well that day and he got to know what I did too. I invited him to come over to my office—"if you're interested in checking out a bright future," I added. One month later I hired him and he joined our company. Naturally, my partners were mystified. "But he's only twenty-three, Jim, he's just a kid," said one. "No real business experience, no executive search experience, no track record, no selling experience, no knowledge of computers," said the other, continuing, "not a great student—a philosophy major to boot!"

Putting together a rotation plan so that my team could help him develop fundamentals while working on short, low-risk assignments, I prescribed readings, company visits, and other ways Will could come up to speed. I tried to remove as many obstacles for him as possible in the organization.

I also had him work with me on one of the toughest client assignments in the shop, a search for a rare engineering leader to work in a young company doing computer simulations in molecular biology. This client was tough to please and under a lot of pressure to get its products to market. Though his first few weeks were refreshing and full of excitement, this new project signaled to Will how much of a challenge his new career was really going to be.

With encouragement and coaching, he plugged away at the research we needed to do on the project, calling contacts and candidates, and facing, in the process, a lot of rejection. More than once in these early days, he confided to me that he wasn't sure he was cut out for this kind of work. "I like having more outside contact with people." He said, "All this telephone research gets to me."

Setting aside some other priorities, I worked more closely with him for the next few weeks. Getting to know his wife Brenda and learning about their dreams of buying a house and starting a family, I also learned from Will that he had been an only child whose father was an M.D., and that he'd been "over-protected" by his parents growing up. Although a very social creature with lots of friends and interests, he'd never really excelled at anything and apparently tended to avoid putting out extraordinary efforts at work. He had always preferred instead, to emphasize other, more personal interests. It became clear to me that he feared, or was skeptical of, a business career.

Despite these drawbacks, Will helped me solve the difficult engineering-leader project (we found the perfect candidate for our client company), and this victory afforded him a measure of some much-needed confidence and a real feel for the successful side of the job. But still, for some reason, he was not really enjoying it yet. I made sure he participated in every company meeting and every client contact that was appropriate for helping him further stimulate his interest, and I had him working on multiple outside assignments as well as internal tasks helping other teams. After a while he seemed to be on the right track, in "fight-not-flight" mode, but still wasn't putting in the long hours to be really successful in this career.

To help him overcome the rough spots, I stayed tuned to his behaviors as best I could and he, in turn, shared with me openly about his feelings and progress. The trust we built during this stage enabled us to discuss and track his strengths and weaknesses, and his development needs. Before long, Will really began to show some promise as he racked up good results.

Professional service firms are high-pressure work environments demanding excellence and fast response times. Six months into Will's employment, he hit the wall. The work environment still didn't feel right to him, his peers on other teams—unaccustomed to filling a coaching role-stopped being much help to him, and I watched his performance and motivation take a steep dive. My partners wanted me to fire him. Staff professionals thought he was too slow to learn. One senior partner told me, "Jim, he's a likeable kid but lacks brainpower." I knew, of course, that this was not true, knowing as I did how far he had come, and how he had excelled at much of his work. Now it was getting spotty and had to be corrected—or else.

Time for a serious discussion. I still believed in him but I had to identify his drop-off in performance and motivation and the fact that he was losing the confidence of his peers. For his part, although he now understood what a clearly lucrative field this was for those who succeeded in it, he also knew that he would never be one of the leaders if he couldn't regroup and resume achieving his goals.

At first Will's response to my questions was to retreat. "I'm thinking of moving out of state, to be near my parents," he said. "I might like to try to find work as a teacher at a private school or something. I'm just not sure I'm cut out for this kind of work—it's too hard."

My response to him was pretty direct. I had to sincerely use every coaching technique I knew. I decided to share my own struggle. " Will, you may think this business came easy for me, but it didn't. There were lots of times I looked for a way out, to find something easier to do. I didn't even like the business world at first, and I didn't start liking it until I began to see its value to people. I can tell you that ever since I decided to stay in this business that I've become a better person for it. And my family has enjoyed the benefits of that, too."

I now brought him back to his own experiences. "Will, you remember how happy you were when the last two clients thanked us for solving their searches?" I disclosed some other challenges I had faced during a similar point in my career and how it had all been worth it in the end to "find a way, make a way," to creatively satisfy my clients. I sensed him beginning to relax as he recognized that even a top person in this field could have once had the same problems.

That display of confidence in him proved important. "Will, you now know how to do this kind of work, you're good with clients, you're learning a lot and you're working in a highly professional environment with great pay, good people, and a real future. You have seen how we can positively impact people's careers in our work and positively affect their companies. You also insist that you enjoy helping people. By all counts, this seems like exactly the right place for you to be at this moment in your life. So help me understand what's wrong with this picture, why doesn't it feel right to *you?*"

Here now are a few of the pointed questions I asked Will during our discussion. I attempted to ask these questions in only the most supportive way I could, aiming to challenge him and break him out of his downward spin.

▲ "I'm puzzled about your motivation dropping off so much in the last two months despite your doing so well for so long. Can we talk about what's changed?"

▲ "Will, I sense that you are retreating when you should be charging ahead. What's the downside of giving this a full effort? Are you having trouble with all this responsibility?"

▲ You agree that you aren't giving your best effort. Whatever work you choose, don't you owe it to yourself and to your family to do the best that you can? What's stopping you from proving here and now that you can excel at something?"

These questions were designed to not only support Will and bring out his issues but to challenge his thinking on them as well. If I could get him talking freely, without reacting defensively, we could get to the core of his problems. Only in that way might he break through them and regain his momentum and motivation.

Fortunately, in this case, it worked! With a little more discussion, Will admitted he was feeling as if he had entered a long tunnel with no side doors. Getting on a career track with a house, a mortgage, and a family terrified him. Very much in love with his wife, he didn't want to disappoint her, but he was afraid. By getting him talking about his fears, we got to the heart of the matter.

"Everybody gets overwhelmed at times," I confided, " but the real issue is commitment. You've already admitted that too many times in your life you have not given it your best. Since you already made the commitment here, and to your wife, maybe now it's time for you to follow-through. Is it an option to let Brenda down?" Will shook his head no.

I decided to put a challenge to him "Here is what we should do, Will: I am going to support you one-hundred percent for the next four months. However, in return I want one-hundred percent back from you. Demonstrate anything less than that and I'll let you move on to whatever else you want. I am going to measure you only against your applying yourself one-hundred percent. It's OK to make mistakes; I don't care what anyone else thinks as long as you're trying your best. But I also know how much better you will feel about your work if you take this challenge." I added one last thing. "I want you to talk to Brenda tonight about all I've just said. Let me know your thoughts in the morning. If you and she don't agree with my plan for you, I'll write you out a severance check that will help your transition from here be a little easier and we'll part friends."

The next morning Will came back with a new fire in his belly and renewed conviction. Midday, Brenda called to tell me she agreed with me completely. "Will's problem is he has to overcome his fears and make the commitment to apply himself as a business person who can make a difference," she said. "And now, thanks to your intervention, I know he will." And it was true. Will began applying himself that very day to become "the best he could be" and within six months we promoted him to a new position and since that time has never stopped growing. Over the next several years, he continued growing, producing for the firm at the highest levels and winning VP status by the time he was thirty. He and Brenda now have two beautiful children and he continues to thrive in his work and enjoy it as he simultaneously coaches and develops "younger" recruits.

By painting a picture of a business future that fit what he really cared about, Will finally was able to engage himself fully and make a powerful new commitment to everyone important in his life- co-workers, superiors, me, our clients, his wife Brenda and, perhaps most importantly—himself.

KEY COACHING SKILLS

You can see from all the ups and downs that permeated my coaching of Will, there are many minefields to be traversed and challenges to meet. Coaching succeeds when performed skillfully. The following five ways of acting bring maximum coaching effectiveness. They are:

1. ATTEND—While actively listening, convey to your coachee you are really hearing him/her through verbal ("I see," "OK," "Yes, I agree"), vocal ("mmm", "ah ha", vocal sounds) and nonvocal means (keeping eye contact, nodding). Body language indicating keen attention and openness with a relaxed pose while facing the other squarely is important.

2. INQUIRE—Use open and closed questions and directives to develop sufficient information. Examples: (open question) "What do you think about the current project plan?"; (closed question) "Do you think it is aggressive enough?"; (open directive) "Tell me how the deadline can be brought in by a week"; (closed directive) "Will you be relying on Gary to ensure this objective?"

3. REFLECT—When a coach "plays back" what he or she has heard, he/she ensures an understanding what the coachee has been

saying. Repeat or rephrase your coachee's words: "You're saying that the resources are insufficient to make the new deadline?"

4. **CONFRONT**—Used sparingly, challenging and confronting allows the coach, among many other benefits, to keep coachees on track and provide them with discipline by pointing out discrepancies between commitments, words, and actions. "On the one hand you say you want to be on the executive committee but on the other, I don't see your concern for productivity gains or improvements in cycle time in our planning sessions. Help me understand this disconnect."

5. **AFFIRM**—Frequent verbal reinforcing increases the coachee's sense of competency and willingness to tackle tough problems. Example: "Thanks for helping me see the rest of the picture— together we have made some progress today. I feel that you have now identified a policy change and several bottlenecks and are able to utilize the current resources you now have to complete this project within the new time frame. I will also support you in the policy change."

PLAN YOUR FEEDBACK

It has been said that feedback is the breakfast of champions. To ensure that your feedback is effective, follow these simple criteria: Your feedback must be timely, specific, reasonable and constructive in intent. That's the "Golden Rule" of feedback.

How can you be sure your feedback meets the Golden Rule? How can you know that it covers criteria required for positive feedback, such as the five key coaching skills? Finally, how can you set the stage for ultimately achieving the desired shape of an effective coaching moment?

The answer is to *plan* your feedback. By paying attention to eight critical feedback-planning steps, you maximize your coaching moment's chances of success. You have structured a process; you're not just rambling or winging it. The coaching moment process becomes precise and businesslike.

The eight feedback-planning steps are:

1. First, write out your personal objective for this coaching.

2. Next, be prepared to drop your own agenda and write out the shared objective, i.e., the coaching's business purpose.

3. Decide your "approach." How do you want to begin this coaching process, how will you tailor it to your coachee's style and needs?

4. Describe current behaviors, that is, list/examine behaviors for praise, modification, to build agreement, to compare reality.

5. Specify "in what situations" your coachee's current behaviors (pro and con) have been demonstrated. Draw from data in project plans, activity reports, or other sources.

6. Review impacts and consequences. Here's where you sell the need for change in behavior or continued improvement.

7. Identify alternative behaviors and options. Remember you are coaching, advising, and reviewing solutions, not imposing your own solutions.

8. Reinforce with action statements. Encourage and affirm your coachee's ability to execute the agreed actions that are observable and measurable.

Follow these eight steps and your coaching objectives will be achieved. Great business leaders routinely expand the value of their relationships by conducting coaching in this way.

REVERSE THE ENGINES

So often, managers fail to realize when they are suppressing creativity, growth, learning, and collaboration on their teams. They know how to push a cart but not how to pull one. Would you try to push a two-wheeler with a refrigerator up a set of stairs? Sometimes pulling is a lot more effective—and infinitely easier! For goal-oriented business leaders, coaching is like that, i.e., reversing the engines. It means asking more than telling, shifting at times to "pull management" when "push management" is neither required nor optimal.

Psychologists observe that in relationships, the more one person becomes dominant, the more submissive others in that same environment can become. There is a time for coaching and there is a time for providing direction. The skill comes in recognizing which situation is occurring right now, and then applying the appropriate principles. Too many leaders get themselves stuck in one gear. The real growth principle is to increase one's personal repertoire of responses to human situations in order to obtain the maximum outcomes in the most genuine way.

EXERCISE:

To become more aware of your behaviors and their impact on others, it might help to record in your PowerSkills journal your responses to various coaching dilemmas. Did a situation call for a coaching response to which you should have spent most of your time asking and listening? How did you do? Or did the situation demand a more directing, telling, commanding approach?

By recording what happens when you react to situations, you can learn to evaluate how you are handling critical episodes and adjust your future responses to similar situations accordingly.

DEVELOP THE COACHING HABIT

Whenever you find yourself frustrated with a colleague, partner, or customer, your emotions can be a guide or a destructive force. The first rule for developing the "coaching habit" is often self-management, i.e., reforming yourself. Simply running with the impulse to reform the *other* person will likely be unproductive.

Instead, you want your first instinct to be exploring why *you* are so irritated, or discouraged, or disgusted by this other person's behavior. You may be surprised with what you find, and it may provide a valuable insight into how you might effectively conduct your coaching. Becoming an observer of your own behavior (knowing your own "hot buttons") is one means of maintaining perspective and avoiding playing out your own psychodramas. The shortcut to knowing your hot buttons is to examine your key values, principles that guide your work and life. The next time you are having a conflict with someone, consult the Values Checklist in

Chapter 4 (Positioning) to find out why you are clashing.

Once you have established which key values that are being tested in the relationship, you can ask yourself what past experiences in your personal or business life may be causing you to react or overreact in the present moment. Once your own "head trash" enters the situation your effectiveness as a coach plummets quickly, possibly to zero. We can bring both healthy and/or dysfunctional behaviors from our family life. If we are aware of the choice, we can choose the option that is healthy.

In fact, it turns out that the most stable molecular structure in nature is three particles. In human relationships triangles form naturally, which explains the presence of intermediaries such as counselors, brokers, agents, consultants. This can work well or ill. Often the three roles sort out as "exciter," "amplifier," and "damper." I have observed many situations where emotional triangles among executives fit this description perfectly—sparring partners A and B, and confidante C. Naturally, a good coach or leader doesn't want to get stuck in any of these roles. Being aware of them speaks volumes about how to prevent this. When leaders become coaches, they can break the pattern of such potential triangles that can form throughout a company and prevent growth and change. Since managers constantly gather information about the performance of people in the organization, it is easy to fall into a trap of "Don't ever tell so and so but...". If an employee or a peer comes to you with a complaint about someone else, what is typically your response? "Yeah, I hate the way Bill does that too," you might say, introducing a cycle of toxic destruction to your workplace.

A good coach, however, might respond like this: "Are you sure that Bill intended that?" or "What do you suppose is causing this?" Another way: "Have you ever given Bill some feedback on that?" Such return questions send a powerful message that we all have an obligation to deal with the *sources* of our conflicts. In this way you are also indirectly coaching others to be coaches themselves.

The antidote then for falling back into unhealthy patterns of relating that we may have learned from our families is to practice "no-fault thinking." Getting defensive and finding fault has absolutely no positive business value. When under stress, we at that moment need to be the most vigilant of all about backsliding in this unprofitable direction.

REFORM YOURSELF

Experienced coaches recognize that to be effective as learning leaders, they must reform themselves and become highly self aware.Otherwise, they can bring too much of their own baggage into the process.

▲ RULE #1: Fire Your Critical Parent!

Perhaps the toughest rule for many in this Reform Yourself section is the need to develop a "nurturing parent and nurturing adult" within your psyche. Effective coaching sometimes requires us to get rid of old "tapes," basically inner voices that emanate from (according to Eric Berne's transactional analysis theories) three ego states formed largely in childhood—parent, adult, and child. As business leaders, we too often play out our family-parenting mode even when adult to adult communication is called for. Berne's insight added that we're all capable of operating in what he called "cross transactions" that create conflict. We have all seen, for example, childish behavior come out in an employee when a boss begins acting like a critical parent, invoking as this often does an employee's "rebellious child response."

On the other hand, when a manager takes on the role behavior of a "nurturing" parent (read: "coach"), such a manager will usually win cooperation from his or her employee's adult ego state. Many of us have a "critical parent" running about inside our heads that just won't quit. Once discovered, your "critical parent" can be fired and replaced with a nurturing coach. This may take time and require lots of work in your journal but it *can* be done!

▲ RULE #2: FACE DOWN "INSIGHT WITHOUT ACTION"

Another rule of Reform Yourself is to address the "insight without action" problem. Psychologists who came to us long after Sigmund Freud challenged his notion that after a catharsis a person would automatically change his problem behavior or be freed from a phobic pattern. This, they say, is not necessarily true. In self-destructive behaviors, insight without action can become neurotic. Moving yourself and your clients toward a desired state by confronting your desired versus actual state of things can be a truly empowering approach.

▲ RULE #3: BE YOUR OWN YARDSTICK

▲ RULE #4: CONSERVE ENERGY

These two rules work best when employed together. First, be your own yardstick. Though seeking critical feedback helps us grow, we must also accept ourselves without concern for the judgments of others. This keeps us reality-based and yet still free to be authentic and genuine. By focusing more on your inner reality than on external drivers you concentrate on the possible and have a reserve of energy for yourself and for your important relationships. By comparing yourself with others you can sap all your energy, impairing your judgment and your effectiveness as a leader or a coach. We must be aware of the energy we give and receive from others. This rule can be summed up as: Conserve energy.

Personal renewal and the ability to embrace change is a key to happiness. So finding the right balance can make you strong and healthy. A great coach or guru helps others find such a balance by applying their energies in the right places and directions with a master's skill. These are irresistible qualities for managers to employ in a harried world.

▲ RULE #5: Maintain a Developmental View

You can keep a coach's perspective by viewing others as developing and capable of further growth.

My brother John had always been an all-star athlete, captain of all three major sports in our high school. John could run, shoot, catch, bob, weave, you name it, in whatever sport he tried. In football, in particular, he truly excelled. His football coach was focused on one thing: winning games. With two equally skilled quarterbacks, John and another classmate, Dick Gatly, John's best friend, the coach had a choice to make: Who to play starting quarterback? As John's running and catching abilities were superior to Dick's, he chose John to play wide receiver and Dick to call plays. That was fine on one level: Catching Dick's passes meant John crossed the goal line many times for our team, affording him many touchdowns and much glory.

But at five-foot-ten, John sat on the bench in college while bigger guys over six feet played the starting wide receiver positions. Eventually, out of frustration, John quit the Boston University football team and joined the track team as a sprinter. Back home, many of us wondered whether John's high school coach had done the right thing. Had he played John as a quarterback more in high school would John have ended up a more notable player in college and beyond? Did the coach do the right thing? What was actually his job—to develop his players' potential or to only play those players who could help him win each day's games?

Now in his thirtieth year as a physical education teacher and coach, I asked John on his 55th birthday to reflect on these questions. In typically good-natured style, he said his views on this have evolved over the years. As a young coach, he said, he took the same perspective as his own high school coach did, that winning was everything.

Then he had his own children and his values evolved. Today he focuses more on the development side of the committed players, regardless of the urgings of parents and faculty. He says that, fortunately, he always wins plenty of games anyway, but the thought of holding a kid back is unthinkable to him now, even if it means losing a game here or there. Over the years, he has come to believe that this approach ends up yielding a better program with more loyal support from the community and with kids becoming more committed and motivated. Ironically, or maybe because of John's approach, his teams have had more consistent winning records from year to year than in times past with previous coaches' "winning is everything" philosophies.

A key reason that business leaders and managers fail as coaches is they stop taking a developmental view of their people. Upon labeling someone as "incompetent," "lazy," or "stupid," they stop coaching. Somehow, people think that if they give a person a label, they are off the hook as coaches. In business, while there are unquestionably poor selections of personnel, the majority of workers intrinsically want to learn. Learning, after all, is life.

So when an employee develops a faulty self-appraisal about his capability, it's usually the result of a poor history of feedback. Yes, the employee probably wasn't very proactive in seeking critical feedback either and his self-perception therefore may not be in line with his capabilities. But it's often the company's performance-management system that really provides job-specific performance feedback.

How is yours at your company? Does it (or your coaching approach) allow for coaching employees during all 250 or so official work days of the year, when real events happen, not just once or twice a year on Performance Review Day? Unfortunately, the lack of ongoing feedback in most organizations underlies most terminations. With ongoing coaching (driven by feedback), day-to-day operations, and the resulting bottom-line, can be very different.

The real skill in selecting people for assignments is the ability to recognize their potential. The myth that hiring only proven performers will ensure success is a recipe for overpriced and dysfunctional leadership teams. Proven performers for those assignments often are questing for a new assignment in which they can be tested on a new learning curve. The realistic perspective will be found in seeking out highly talented people with a mix of both proven performance and potential. By taking a long-range perspective, we allow for the possibility that people can grow and that our own skills as a coach will continue to develop.

DEVELOP YOUR INNER COACH

I wish it were otherwise but just reading this book will not change your approach. I wrote earlier about "old tapes" in our heads that can really get in our way, blocking our plans and progress as coaches and business leaders. That's why inner work (introspection) *must* be done to advance your competency in the PowerSkill of coaching.

To give you a chance to take advantage of the "best stuff" inside you, I'd like to introduce you at this point to a powerful visualization exercise. I have used it myself in my efforts to transform myself into a better coach. I invite you to employ it to do the same on your behalf.

EXERCISE:

1. Divide a sheet of paper into three columns titled "Name," "Positive Impact on Me" and "Attributes I Seek."

2. Go back in time to your earliest experiences with family, friends, teachers, coaches, counselors, bosses, and so on. In column #1, name at least five coaches, people who have had a lasting positive impact on you. (You could even list difficult people in your life whose impact, in the end, turned out to be positive.)

3. Write down the most specific positive impacts each person has had on you in column #2.

4. Fill in column #3 by citing the positive attributes you remember about that person that you would like to emulate. Ask yourself too if you can remember any key turning points where these people provided some good coaching or set a positive memorable example for you. (Note: Did you ever thank any of these people? There may still be time, you know. If you make the effort, you'll likely find this to be a rich and rewarding experience.)

5. Review your list of positive attributes from column #3. Can you add one or two additional attributes that make your coach effective or attractive and that you would want to develop for your own inner coach, too?

6. Visualize the image of this "transcendental coach" and the virtues that he or she possesses. Add a fitting name to give your inner coach—possibly use your middle name. Maybe you'll share this name with other people or maybe you'll keep it to yourself. Then find a photo of yourself from a memorable vacation perhaps or in some similar setting where you look relaxed, happy, and wise. Place this photo where you can see it every day. Sign it with your inner coach's name.

Sound silly? Give it a try. I assure you that when you find yourself backsliding into pedestrian behavior, you'll think about your inner coach and ask, "Now what would (your inner coach's name) think or do in this situation?" Before long, you'll be emulating desired behaviors and people will start noticing and responding to you in new ways. After all, these are the "best parts" of you, not some phony you or your dark side. What choice do you make when called upon to summon up one part of yourself or another? Why not indulge in your best talents by calling upon your inner coach?

ESTABLISHING TRUE COACHING RELATIONSHIPS

When you really get good at coaching you'll do it with everyone— customers, friends, your boss, your peers, the rest of upper management. I suggest baby steps first until these new behaviors become natural.

The first step is to become a master of the art of the question, learning to listen with empathy, with what some call a "beginner's mind," that is, free of prejudice and opinions. By developing this skill, you'll simultaneously develop close bonds with people you are coaching. Your interest in them *without judgment* will help you gain insight into their world.

The next step involves recognizing that (a) not everyone is like you and (b) not everyone *should* be like you. In this second step you use that understanding to learn how to adjust your style to be effective with different personalities. The very best thing you can do is develop your "active" listening skills. The more you draw out another person (ideas, objectives, values, approach to decision-making, accomplishments, failures) in a natural and easy style, the less need you have of becoming an "armchair psychologist," guessing at how the other thinks and will behave.

Your intuition will help you adjust your approach. In building the initial rapport, try "mirroring and matching" the person you are communicating with, that is, speaking in a low, slow tone if that is his way of speaking, sitting in a similar position, smiling often if that is this person's way. Such mirror/match behavior works well with empathetic listening. At some point in the conversation you begin to initiate your own style and you will find the person mirroring you.

But this does not mean being disingenuous or agreeing with everything the person says, especially with things you do not believe yourself. By emulating another's style you can lower his/her defenses as you begin bringing more of your own style into the situation. By flexing your communication styles, you also "imprint" in your mind the most effective methods of communicating with this same person in the future.

PERSONALITY TYPING

While putting labels on people can be a surefire way to lose your developmental perspective, many personality-typing systems can nonetheless help you understand your basic style and that of others. Each of us has a basic personality style that comes out, particularly when we are under stress. But by using techniques like developing an "inner coach" I believe we're also capable of evolving beyond type. In fact, the most developed lifelong learners seem to defy categorization as a static "type," evolving a great many different ways of responding and initiating with others.

From my experience, the most widely accepted personality-type instrument in business is the Myers-Briggs Type indicator (MBTI). But what tends to happen, I've observed, is that many people who take a workshop on a personality typing or mapping scheme tend to forget the particular system quickly, or acquire understanding of only one system. This causes them to develop a very narrow viewpoint on relationships because they attempt to put everyone in one of their system's "boxes." What's needed instead is a way to interpret behavior in real time. Since we obviously can't require our clients to take a personality inventory, and as guessing about personality can be misleading and even dangerous, active listening and keen observation will remain as the best practice. Simply by gathering information on key people you will obtain your best information about them from people who work (or have worked) with them day in and day out.

The Enneagram

Having said that, I'd like to share one personality typing system with you that I feel is unique. I like it because it's easy to remember, fast, requires no certifications or licensing, and has been around (and used) for over 24 centuries. Known as the Enneagram, it was rediscovered and interpreted over the past 25 years by a number of contemporary psychologists, academicians, and clergy. Helen Palmer and Don Richard Riso, the two prominent researchers, practitioners, and authors in this field have traced the roots of the Enneagram to ancient oral traditions but agree that its exact origin remains a mystery. For those interested in learning more about the Enneagram, I strongly recommend Helen Palmer's book, *The Enneagram in Love and Work* and Don Richard Riso's *Understanding the Enneagram*. I have found their descriptions of the interactions of the types in relationships extremely helpful in pinpointing my own style and enabling me to reflect upon better ways to coach others very different from myself. Herb Pearce, a colleague, educator, and psychotherapist, is an expert on personality-typing systems and uses them in his workshops. Pearce's overview of the system is worth noting here along with some of its implications for coaching. "The Enneagram is a personality system that describes nine attentional styles, very useful in business, as well as personal relationships. More and more companies are using it in their training and coaching needs."

Here's an adapted description of each type, some hints on their development and Herb's suggestions on how to relate to them effectively.

▶ THE ENNEAGRAM TYPES

TYPE #1: The Perfectionist

▶ The Perfectionist strives for perfection and constant improvement, tends to be critical both of self and others, has strong moral values and believes that there's a right or best way to do everything. This coachee needs to learn flexibility and notice what's right as much as what's wrong. In working with Type 1s, be on time, communicate strong values, encourage them to have fun, give them permission to make mistakes, admit your own mistakes, acknowledge their integrity, commitment and precision, be clear, and don't make promises you can't keep.

TYPE #2: The Helper

▶ The Helper notices and meets the needs of others though can often get over-involved in helping. Tends to be upbeat and creates the best impression no matter what the situation. This coachee needs to focus more on his/her own needs and make it easier for others to give, too. Must be more direct about what he/she wants. In working with Type 2s, appreciate their giving, give to them without their asking, don't complain too much, be enthusiastic, support them to identify their needs, and acknowledge ways they affect you positively.

THE ENNEAGRAM TYPES (continued)

TYPE #3: The Performer/Achiever

▶ The Performer/Achiever is efficient, bottom-line, task-driven, goal-oriented. Often praised, but exhausted. Instead of competing to win or doing too much of the work alone, must learn to be a team player, ask for help and realize improving relationships is as important as, and often contributes to, results. In working with Type 3s, be clear and to the point, talk about goals, let them support you in your goals, acknowledge their material giving and their ideas for practical action, acknowledge how the results they produce affect you personally, give them ideas to help produce results.

TYPE #4: The Individualist

▶ The Individualist is focused on being unique and independent, has emotional flair, is creative and aesthetically inclined. Could learn to fit into the "norm" a bit more, avoid creating office theatrics, and do more to support others and focus outside themselves. In working with Type 4s, be passionate about life, appreciate their depth of feeling, appreciate their creativity, set limits for yourself in relating to them, accept mood swings as normal, support their artistic side, and don't try to get them to conform.

TYPE #5: The Observer

▶ The Observer is inspired by knowledge and information, excited about ideas often more than people. Tends to be private, annoyed by intrusion, can be engaged by the sharing of mutually interesting subjects. Can leave others guessing. Must become more self-revealing and sharing of process needs. In working with Type 5s, explain things, be specific, get to the point and don't repeat, give them time to think and time to make decisions, be clear about your expectations, don't expect personal sharing, be objective and direct but not aggressive, expect their feelings to held more privately.

▶ THE ENNEAGRAM TYPES (continued)

TYPE #6: The Questioner

▶ **The Questioner** questions everything, tends to be skeptical and doubting, yet very loyal to people when they are honest and loyal. Prepares in advance. Must learn to focus on the positive as well as the negative and watch tendency to project parts of self onto others. In working with Type 6s, expect preparation and thorough thinking before action, give them time to share doubts and problems, let them fix or solve things they're good at, be aware of their need to feel part of a group.

TYPE #7: The Optimist

▶ **The Optimist** sees the best-case scenario in every situation, loves ideas, possibilities, and the bright side. Also loves to start new things and have fun but moves on quickly as soon as routine sets in. Must learn to complete things or get help and not avoid reality. In working with Type 7s, be positive, don't expect them to listen to your pain for long; brainstorm ideas, laugh, get excited, do new things, be spontaneous.

TYPE #8: The Challenger

▶ **The Challenger** often the boss, likes to be in control and take charge, say or do what he or she wants. Has difficulty understanding why others don't do the same. Must learn to be more patient, less impulsive, and more open to, and revealing of, hidden insecurities. In working with Type 8s, be direct, say what you need and what you want, be action based; expect directness, fast action, and impatience.

TYPE #9: The Peacemaker

▶ **The Peacemaker** often the mediator at work, tries to calm and sooth other's internal and external conflicts—can't stand conflict! Must learn to focus more on own self and own goals and realize conflict is a natural consequence of differences. In working with Type 9s, be patient and kind, expect ambivalence, validate and support their assertiveness, ask if they need help regarding decision-making, expect fear and withholding regarding conflict, support them in clarifying goals and support them to action.

THE SEVEN FACES OF RESISTANCE

As a manager when coaching for improved performance, be prepared to meet resistance. One or more of the following often arise early in a coaching process in one form or another, so be ready! Without great vigilance on the part of the coach, these "seven faces of resistance" can block out truly effective coaching and feedback every time:

1. "That is not a problem" (general denial)
2. "Not enough time" (poor time management)
3. "Our business is different" (uniqueness syndrome)
4. "Not a priority now" (priority mismatch)
5. "Management won't support it" (victimhood)
6. "I don't know enough." "I can't..." (passive behavior)
7. "We don't have enough resources." (weak project management)

Are they reasons or excuses? Great coaches quickly see these possible roadblocks and use their inquiring, reflecting, and confronting skills to identify their truth or falsity.

CHAPTER KEY POINTS

▲ Coaching holds the key to operating business relationship networks effectively and deepens them.

▲ You don't have to enter into a formal coaching relationship to coach and be coached.

▲ Coaching is the best way to create learning relationships all around you.

▲ Coaching is a relationship-builder, reinforcing your desired positioning.

▲ To be effective as a coach, each of us must commit ourselves to genuine self-development.

▲ Coaching may be used for problem solving, to improve a direct report's performance, or to assist another's process of personal transformation.

▲ Five skills in particular enable maximum coaching effectiveness: attend, inquire, reflect, confront, and affirm.

▲ Plan your feedback to make it effective and make it timely, specific, reasonable, and constructive in intent.

▲ The first rule for developing the coaching habit is self-management, i.e., reforming yourself.

▲ Effective coaching may require getting rid of old "tapes."

▲ When we get really good at coaching we do it with everyone—customers, bosses, upper management, colleagues, friends, family.

QUESTIONS FOR YOUR POWERSKILLS JOURNAL

▲ Are you a trusted advisor and mentor to your internal and external clients?

▲ Are you a coaching resource to your Nifty Fifty?

▲ Do you employ coaching, asking, and active listening to create empowered relationships?

▲ Have you successfully established stretch goals as part of your coaching of individuals and teams?

PRACTICE TIPS

▲ In the next three weeks, identify a specific coaching opportunity and a coaching goal with someone that already sees you as a mentor. Practice four of the five key coaching skills—attending, inquiring, reflecting, and affirming in developing information and developing alternatives. Follow up to see if the agreed-upon behavior is implemented.

▲ Now try a more challenging situation in which you need to provide some challenging feedback and may need to constructively confront some behavior of a subordinate or coworker. Use the eight steps for planning your feedback to prepare yourself for the confronting aspect of the coaching session. How did you meld the five coaching skills in the interaction?

▲ Partner up with a trusted friend or colleague that knows you well to exchange views on your personal "blocks" to effective coaching. What is preventing you from being in the coaching mode or doing it well?

▲ Consider taking a course on coaching skills and expanding your readings in this area.

RESOURCES

Click on **www.powerskills.com/coaching** for readings, links, courseware and resources to develop this skill.

The Executive as Coach, James Waldroop and Timothy Butler. Boston: Harvard Business Review, November-December 1996.

Listening: The Forgotten Skill by Madelyn Burley-Allen. New York, NY: John Wiley & Sons, Inc., 1995. ISBN 0-471-01587-3

Masterful Coaching by Robert Hargrove. San Francisco: Jossey-Bass Pfeiffer Printing, 1995. ISBN 0-89384-281-8

The Tao of Coaching: Boost Your Effectiveness at Work by Inspiring Those Around You by Max Landsberg. Santa Monica, CA: Knowledge Exchange, LLC, 1997. ISBN 1-888232-34-X

CHAPTER 7

POWERSKILL #4: LEADING

"With the best of leaders,
When the work is done,
The project completed,
The people all say,
'We did it ourselves.'"

—Lao-tzu

When he joined McKinsey and Company in 1933, management attorney Marvin Bower could've just towed the line and done exactly what others who had joined the young firm before him had done. At that time, McKinsey had only been around for eight years, one of a plethora of engineering and management firms that had sprouted up after Fredrick Winslow Taylor's thought revolution just before World War I. "Consulting" firms then did pretty much what the client company asked—solved an engineering dilemma, took care of the client's accounting needs, basing their approaches on the functional, operational, orderly principles of Taylor's theories of "scientific management."

But Bower came to Chicago, McKinsey's base, with a mind of his own, influenced chiefly by his Harvard Business School training and recent years spent at a Cleveland law firm. He had been responsible for restructuring faltering companies, saving them from the ravages of the double whammy of the Crash and the Great Depression. This work Bower found "much more interesting," he admitted years later, "than anything I had been doing in the law." His charge had been to advise companies on how they could get back on their feet, and how their managements must operate if they were to succeed again.

In the process of analyzing and making recommendations, Bower found that if he always met his client's needs first, even when it meant clashing with the wishes of his own employer, the right outcome would always emerge and everyone would end up happy. He brought the same outlook and standards to McKinsey, where, rather than relying on a slide rule or a tabulator, he rolled out a new tool called an organizational chart. With this, he was able to broadly analyze McKinsey client problems, explain to client executives such concepts as delegation, accountability, and authority flow, and outline how to integrate professional and ethical standards with management decision-making processes. Without this last, he maintained, his clients, in the long run, would not succeed.

The Bower way ultimately not only transformed how McKinsey and Company conducted its business but also set the stage for the practice of management consulting as we know it today. By his own account, Bower, now 95, has said that leading McKinsey down a path of operating from the highest professional standards ultimately determined its market dominance and mega-success. Recently he listed these standards as he now sees them in *The Will to Lead*, published by Harvard Business School Press (1997):

▲ Put client interest ahead of firm interests.

▲ Adhere to the highest standards of truthfulness, integrity, and trustworthiness.

▲ Maintain in confidence the private and proprietary information of client organizations and any sensitive opinions of individuals within client organizations.

▲ Maintain an independent position, being ready to differ with client executives and to tell them the truth as we see it, even though that may adversely affect firm income or endanger continuance of the relationship.

▲ Provide services in which the firm is competent and that provide full value for the client.

The topic of leadership has been given the most ink by business writers. Leadership programs are also the most demanded management education programs. The use of the term leading here is specific to its use in the management and operation of relationship networks—the kind of leadership we think of when we talk about "leading by influence." The best way to introduce our fourth PowerSkill may be to simply state that the most effective leaders in any walk of life are usually those who exercise leadership naturally, incorporating it into their lives as a "way of being." What does this mean to those of us who don't come by such talents easily? From my vantage point, great business leaders always take responsibility for not only managing relationships but also serving as a role model for them. They also bring who they are into what they do, holding on so closely to their personal beliefs that no one can push their momentum off the mark. Had Marvin Bower simply gone along with the conventional job expectations of consultants of his day, that profession, and the value it has since delivered to countless companies over six decades, would never have been developed.

In fact, we can only imagine how Marvin's detractors might have viewed or treated him back then, the clients that didn't appreciate his recommending hard changes, the colleagues at McKinsey who would've preferred to stay with their comfortable, narrowly beneficial tasks. Yet Marvin plunged on, battling (in his words) "the horrors of hierarchy," taking the reigns of McKinsey in 1935 (when the company's namesake James O. McKinsey moved on to other things) and building it into the international powerhouse it is today.

The PowerSkill of personal leadership inspires others in other ways too, by tendering, for example, "conditional positive regard." This means that when someone has been operating at the upper reaches of their professional capabilities, true leaders acknowledge them visibly, with recognition and respect. Unconditional positive regard on the other hand can lead to the setting of low standards. Recall, for example, the very best teacher you ever had in school. I'll bet that whoever comes to mind was also a tough grader or assigned lots of homework or kept the spotlight on you in class when you were asked a question. Expecting excellence from themselves and others represents a hallmark of great leaders, whether we mean teachers, CEOs, project administrators, or anyone else in a position of authority.

Leadership and management may in fact be inherently at odds. Folks who like to "manage" that is, exercise so-called command-and-control methods, don't tend to succeed in environments that demand creativity, flexibility, excitement, that is, in the basic environment of any leading organization today. True leaders instead engage you with their initiative; they are willing to dig right in and get things jelling without being asked. Today, when even the largest companies strive for such entrepreneurial energy, more traditional management styles are becoming less prevalent as get-up-and-go personal leadership style has become the expected approach.

PERSONAL LEADERSHIP MODEL

At this point, let's define personal leadership by putting it under a PowerSkills microscope. Our PowerSkills definition will not be the traditional one found in most management or business books. The perspective of such books may be right on the money for functional leaders and managers but it does not directly speak to us in the context of personal leadership in peer-to-peer relationships. The "classic" functions of leadership are in the following areas: providing vision, leading teams, holding people accountable, satisfying customers, developing human resources, managing work processes, managing change, and measuring performance.

Not all professionals are specifically responsible for these as a job function. Consider truly successful people in today's organizations. Such individuals thrive while serving on multiple teams, orchestrating multiple projects, and juggling as well the triple roles of leader, contributor, and supporter, often to many of the same people over the course of the same week. Collaboration matters to today's personal leaders. Titles have all but slipped away to an irretrievable irrelevancy.

At an "all-hands meeting" that I facilitated for a young software company, its executive, technical, and sales teams and I worked out ways to conceptualize and formulate a template for personal leadership. We explored vision, mission, values, plans, alignment, and measurements as well as how each executive might provide more personal leadership in every corner of the new organization. Upon completing this exercise, we quickly saw that effective personal leadership is all about how we manage ourselves, our projects, and our relationships.

Multifaceted in every way, leading succeeds in proportion to our roles or intentions. Here are a few examples of how one's leadership goals might play out, depending on the purpose they are intended to serve:

▲ Self-Management Intention: "I will be known as an active listener and solicit feedback from my peers to improve my performance."

▲ Project-Management Intention: "I will energize and identify ways for my project team to accelerate cycle time."

▲ Relationship-Management Intention: "I will create several advocates from my past relationships that will help our company."

Can you see how role and intention can affect the goals you might set for yourself? Once you have explored your key values and goals, and the vision, mission, values, plans, alignment, and measurements of your team, you can use a flip chart to put together a personal leadership model in a list format. For an example, Archer Development evolved such a template after the experience of guiding several client companies through this brainstorming exercise. Take a look at the following Personal Leadership Model, Exhibit 7.1. Another group may come up with different words to describe these personal leadership qualities, but the process brings a team a clarity of thinking while participating in the exercise.

▶ **EXHIBIT 7.1 Personal Leadership Model**

ATTITUDE A feeling or emotion toward a fact or state

- ▶ Positive energy
- ▶ Pursuit of shared vision & values
- ▶ Passion for customers
- ▶ Striving for continuous improvement
- ▶ Curiosity to know the business
- ▶ Accepting ownership/ accountability
- ▶ Embracing change
- ▶ Overcoming obstacles: Find a way/make a way
- ▶ No excuses: results matter
- ▶ Respect for people, their time, and capabilities

BEHAVIOR The manner of conducting oneself

- ▶ Take initiative to advance the business
- ▶ See the big picture, think ahead
- ▶ Prioritize/drive projects to timely closure
- ▶ Follow through on commitments
- ▶ Diagnose/address issues early
- ▶ Share lessons learned, mistakes made
- ▶ Stewardship: effectively utilize resources and time
- ▶ Effectively balance process and results
- ▶ Always be developing your successor(s)
- ▶ Go the extra mile

COMMUNICATION A process by which information is exchanged between individuals through a common system

- ▶ Be active listeners
- ▶ Cards up – Fangs in!
- ▶ Publish your plans
- ▶ Build consensus as appropriate
- ▶ Solicit/give feedback
- ▶ Communicate project status to all stakeholders
- ▶ No surprises

As you read through these lists, can you see how much leading is really about initiating? Simply responding to relationships (or resisting them) both saps our energy and causes us to take responsibility for matters we should actually be delegating. Sometimes we should be delegating to our staff, of course, and other times to a peer or even to our boss. Sometimes we should even be delegating back to our client! If we don't take the time to analyze what needs to be done, and assume responsibility for somehow getting it done, we'll often end up just doing what someone else thinks should be done and never thinking through our own priorities. Leadership means thinking ahead and setting your ideas in motion.

Unlike some of the more specialized skills, (i.e., positioning, hunting or coaching) leading is about will and mindset. Once you've defined it mentally, leading is more about will than skill. Sometimes, just being willing to jump in and offer your help in a situation where you know you can add value to your VIRs, based upon your knowledge or abilities, is the best way to demonstrate your personal leadership.

CLOSED-LOOP DELEGATION

Effective leadership involves follow-through. People around you need to understand that you mean business—defining problems, developing solutions, distributing tasks, and following up on agreements made. We can expect what we inspect, and it is true that people that respect us will generally do what we expect of them—especially if we negotiate actions with dates and *write them down.* They have to know, as in Arnold Schwarznegger's famous line from the movie, *The Terminator,* "I'll be back."

Many people will protest, of course, insisting they are so stressed by the demands of their current job they simply have no time or energy, let alone power, to assume such control. When we expend energy in such resistance, however, we miss the point, and we miss glaring opportunity. Paradoxically, by changing the context within which we view our roles we can empower ourselves to get *more* done, faster, and with much less stress. By failing to leverage the people around us, we miss out on this opportunity, on transforming our lives (for the better!). Grab such opportunity, however, and the world beats a path to your door!

PERSONAL LEADERSHIP: NO PERMISSION REQUIRED

Recall when you gained mastery over an activity or a skillset? Ever made a New Year's resolution that you vowed you would absolutely keep?

Just being able to make a commitment to yourself and follow through with it provides the strength to do so many other things. Gaining mastery over a bad habit or developing a positive new one can also be very empowering.

For example, many years ago, management consultant Ethel Cook started out in her career as an executive secretary. In one of her early jobs, she had been the project organizer of an in-house management conference that her boss had asked assigned to her. This conference required the bringing together of company executives from the far-flung reaches of the organization, and logistically had not been an easy event to pull off, but nonetheless Ethel had achieved it.

On the day of the conference, just before it was about to begin, Ethel's boss, rightly impressed by what she had done, wanted to acknowledge her.

"I'm going to introduce you at the beginning and credit you for this grand day," he told her. "You don't have to make a speech or anything, just stand up and say a few words, then sit down. I just want you to get some credit."

Although for many of us this gesture would come as a pleasant surprise, and we would have been grateful for our boss's consideration and appreciativeness, for Ethel her boss's words provoked terror.

"No, I cannot do that," she snapped, "I *will not* do that!"

"But Ethel, what's wrong?" her boss asked innocently.

"I cannot stand up in front of all these people," Ethel replied. "That's not me. I don't like public speaking. I won't do it."

Feebly, Ethel's boss now attempted to explain that she was not being required to "public speak." In fact, if she merely mumbled a thank-you or even nodded her head, that would be sufficient. But to Ethel, the prospect of even such a meek, fleeting public appearance scared her to death and she refused to go along.

"I won't do it, I can't do it, and if you try to make me do it," she said finally, "*I'll quit!*"

At that, her boss naturally "backed down." By no means had he intended to cause such distress in his favorite administrator. Ethel that day did not speak, stand up, or get acknowledged.

Some weeks later, on a bulletin board in the town where she lived, Ethel saw a notice for an organization called Toastmasters, a volunteer-run public-speaking club for those who wanted to practice, and get feedback on, their presentation skills. Remembering the incident with her boss, and her violent reaction to his kind suggestion, she got to wondering: Why was standing up in front of a roomful of even friendly people so terrifying to her? Why had she refused to even try it? What demons had driven her to threaten to quit?

Bravely, Ethel decided to take a first step in a new direction, to change an obviously bad attitude, and perhaps as a result create new, more positive behaviors. Within a week, she had survived her first Toastmasters session, and by the end of the next month, she had successfully attended three more. She had even begun to get up and give short speeches so that, by the end of a year of such new behaviors, she had decided she wanted to become a public speaker!

This decision set her life on a brand new course. Joining the National Speakers Association, she dedicated herself to getting practice as a public speaker wherever and whenever she could. One year, she made it a goal to make 60 appearances that year, at Rotary Clubs, professional groups, adult ed schools—wherever she could. Eventually, she quit her administrative position and opened her own consulting practice, specializing in office organizational issues. To build her practice, she began speaking at association conferences and at companies. She founded an official international professional day called "Do It Day!" and as a result, now gets interviewed annually by media throughout the United States and Canada. In 1997 she served as President of the New England chapter of the National Speakers Association, in effect reaching the opposite end of the scale from that day when she considered quitting a great job rather than getting up in front of a few colleagues to speak.

The power of putting herself on a leadership course had set in motion a new life for Ethel. By making a commitment to erase her bad attitudes, she had then responded by adapting more positive goals. This course of action had repercussions for her everywhere. Needless to say, she has never regretted how it has all turned out.

As you keep Ethel Cook in mind as your inspiration, I ask you now to make a similar resolution to yourself, one that I predict will serve you in a very major way. My request to you is this: Commit yourself to enhancing, every day, your personal leadership. Achieve this by attempting to demonstrate it every day in your interactions with others. This commitment requires no special equipment or practice time outside the scope of your normal activities, though it does, however, ask you to become an observer of your own behavior and to work hard in the direction of mastery. If you take up my challenge, I guarantee you that your efforts, no matter how many ups and downs you encounter along the way, will improve your relationship with your work in three areas: (1) your enjoyment of your work; (2) how well you carry it out; and (3) the sense of meaning your work brings you every day.

THINKING VALUE

Develop a mindset for *thinking value* and you will find that it is your key to exceptional collaborations and to your ability to provide leadership to your VIRs. When you use a combination of your coaching skills and your ability to think value, you will have the very best way to generate what psychologists call a state of "flow." In this frame of mind, you become so absorbed in what you are doing that you forget everything else and pay unlimited, undivided attention to the task or relationship at hand.

Many of us recognize that athletes and musicians frequently experience this state of being fully present, but it can work for us business types, too. As you become more proactive in your relationships you'll begin to notice that you can allow yourself to be spontaneous and serious at the same time and provide leadership in a natural way. This is what I mean by being "in flow in relationships."

If you focus on value exchange in a relationship, that is, what you can offer to a relationship and what it has to offer you, your goals and action planning will become clearer. This makes focus and flow possible. Most of our stress actually comes from focusing on ourselves rather than the task (or relationship) at hand, so if we broaden the way we think of value, we will broaden our relationships and help others achieve satisfying collaborations.

Remember in Chapter 3, The Relationship Equation, when I spoke about being able to deliver a huge amount of added value in one fifteen-minute conversation? By taking into account the calibration, profile, and grouping of each contact, and by thinking value during each and every communication with a VIR, you will be able to do this. A value flow analysis technique that I have developed comes under the following heading, "Ten Values, Ten Powers." By practicing this, you will identify new ways to create value and master this potent PowerSkill, leading.

TEN VALUES, TEN POWERS

When we value something, we give it power. And when we make something powerful, we can deliver concrete results. By keeping in mind more than one possible value exchange at a time, this type of multidimensional collaboration results in a multiplier effect.

There are ten principle value exchanges that can provide us with the means to deliver extraordinary results. Take a look at the following lists of values and powers, Exhibit 7.2, and as you go down the list, brainstorm how you might translate each one into a deliverable for your VIRs. What do you have to offer your clients/customers in each case and what do they have to offer you?

▶ **EXHIBIT 7.2 Ten Values / Ten Powers**

VALUE #1: Economic

- ▶ Power: Financial capital
- ▶ Delivers: Purchasing power, lending capacity, investment capacity
- ▶ Question: What economic advantages can you offer and receive?

VALUE #2: Informational

- ▶ Power: Knowledge
- ▶ Delivers: Business intelligence that offers a competitive edge
- ▶ Question: What information can you ethically offer or receive?

VALUE #3: Political

- ▶ Power: Credibility
- ▶ Delivers: Connects you with key influencers, strong allies, opportunity gateways.
- ▶ Question: How can you help your VIRs access some political clout?

VALUE #4: Ideational

- ▶ Power: Creative
- ▶ Delivers: Fresh ideas, innovation, new product/service applications
- ▶ Question: What new useful concepts can you generate or receive?

VALUE #5: Territorial

▶ **Power:** Presence
▶ **Delivers:** Market reach, target market areas, potential market leadership
▶ **Question:** What new markets can you offer your customers that they need from you, and what can they offer in their customer relationships to you?

VALUE #6: Advisory

▶ **Power:** Strategic
▶ **Delivers:** Timely, informed guidance of your business
▶ **Question:** What strategic counsel can you offer your VIRs that they want or need, and how specifically can they help you in this regard?

VALUE #7: Scientific

▶ **Power:** Technological
▶ **Delivers:** Competitive advantages from specialized systems, patents, copyrights, methodologies
▶ **Question:** What process improvements or techniques can you share?

VALUE #8: Promotional

▶ **Power:** Public relations and media
▶ **Delivers:** Widened public/market awareness of your product, services, and company; enhanced positive image
▶ **Question:** How can you offer to create for your VIRs the visibility that they desire and how can your customers help you broaden your public relations?

VALUE #9: Social

▶ **Power:** Associative
▶ **Delivers:** Rewarding educational, cultural, recreational, business, and networking affiliations and events
▶ **Question:** What events can you share with your VIRs?

VALUE #10: Inspirational

▶ **Power:** Motivation
▶ **Delivers:** High energy, positive mindsets, commitment
▶ **Question:** How can you encourage and energize your VIRs to deal with their challenges? How might they reciprocate?

Don't worry about getting wrong answers. An exercise such as this one takes practice. But the more you brainstorm, the more you'll be thinking value. The point is to get yourself thinking about how much value you truly offer to others and what kind of power such value creates. You use this power to help others (VIRs/clients/customers in this case) and you look for ways to gain something from them in return. We're talking business relationships here, remember, so it is absolutely all about give-and-take.

To summarize, when you get really good at thinking and collaborating in terms of the Ten Values/Ten Powers the process will become second nature. Too often we narrowly focus on economic value and miss the nine other ways to mutually create value with clients. You will at times operate along the entire spectrum all at once. Self-empowerment, and win-win relationship management like this is very satisfying.

COLLABORATIVE LEADERSHIP AND YOUR NIFTY FIFTY

Essentially there are four ways (styles) that business people manage their relationship networks. The highest energy and long term payoff is generally the collaborative-leadership style. Becoming a collaborator with broad and deep relationships is a choice that we can make and requires some discipline in each of the powerskills. Doing a Nifty Fifty analysis accurately pinpoints how you manage your networks and the kind of relationship power and influence you develop. Exhibit 7.3 shows the four management styles; then each style is described in more detail.

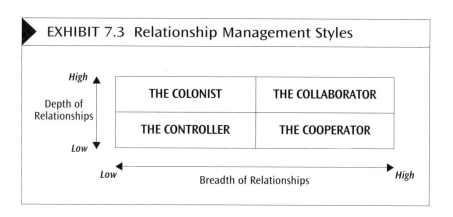

EXHIBIT 7.3 Relationship Management Styles

The Collaborator: High-depth / High-breadth of VIRs

Enjoys many personalized relationships in which value on many levels is exchanged. Open to possibilities and new relationships. Sees relationships as an asset and managing them as a primary activity. Has a multidimensional view and approach to relationships. Has trouble creating a list of only fifty. Probably could identify several lists with many groupings around shared interests. Because the collaborator is perceived to have value and power, people with other styles are attracted to such a manager. Collaborators have learned how to manage by influence and not position power.

The Colonist: High-depth / Low-breadth of VIRs

Enjoys loyal relationships with a few special people by choice or disposition. Might limit close relationships to a few friends, family, and business associates. Stakes out the territory and does not go out of the circle often. May be transactional and task-oriented with people outside a close circle.

The Cooperator: Low-depth / High-breadth of VIRs

Tends to have a just-in-time approach to relationships. Sees utility in cooperating with others as a way to accomplish tasks. Could be an active networker with task energy as the driver or one who responds to requests and is service-oriented. Does not tend to think longer term or strategically about relationships—more of a "cooperate and graduate" approach. May have many enjoyable social relationships.

The Controller: Low-depth/Low-breadth of VIRs

Relationships are a means to an end; challenges to be solved, can be inconvenient, sometimes best avoided and sometimes manipulated. The controller may view relationships as competitions to be won, and could be a win-lose negotiator. Transactions are more important than relationships regardless of what they say. May enjoy business success from time to time even at the expense of long-term relationships. Deals and personal agendas are more important. As a manager, relies heavily on position power.

INSPIRING OTHERS

It is simple, really. During the course of any given business day, people oscillate between fear and greed, worrying about what could go wrong while wanting to benefit as much as they can from an experience or opportunity. You could call it their "flight or fight responses."

Excellence lies in appealing to the potential of collaborative partnership to achieve something for the greater good. Appealing to the motivation for excellence sets you apart. You only bounce between those extremes of fear and greed if you allow it or you reinforce it in others. Fear craves company, greed loathes company, excellence enjoys company. If you want to inspire others, focus your discussions on achieving excellence.

Yet leaders require both respect and results. Conflict is the stimulus for growth, not a dynamic to necessarily avoid. On the other hand, we have all met executives who never met a battle they didn't like, mistaking personal attacks for "constructive" confrontation. Great business leaders instead contribute to the success of others by validating their sense of well-being and self-esteem.

While the "invalidators" work on a pulley system, i.e., pulling themselves up while lowering others down, true leaders resolve conflict in three very positive ways:

1. By knowing what they want. Whenever we know what we want out of a situation we're much more relaxed and in control.

2. By finding out what the other person wants. This kind of inquiry helps make the other party feel understood.

3. By finding common ground and proposing win-win solutions. These will result in actions the other person can accept.

You can see that great business leaders have a knack for turning seeming negatives into positives. This is beneficial for everyone because, in general, people love to be around other people leaders who validate them even when they disagree or are locked in battle over issues and strategies. Knowing how to validate others represents a powerful leading skill.

There are four main actions great leaders employ regularly to validate others:

1. Active empathetic listening (emphasized in the previous chapter)
2. Respecting the other's time
3. Reinforcing and recognizing their positives
4. Challenging them to do better

OVERCOMING THE EGO

A key to leading others well is to stay as far away from role identification as possible and focus wholly on goals. When we get caught up in roles, titles, status—ego, actually—we lose all perspective. Kings and presidents have fallen more than once because they started to believe their own press. If you really want to get things accomplished, if you truly care about the job you have been selected to do, if you want to maintain loyal, motivated, dedicated troops, get your ego out of it and stay focused on group goals and your potential contributions.

To keep goal focused and your ego in check, frequently ask yourself the following questions:

▲ What's the main objective for this project?

▲ How would I like to contribute to it?

▲ How can I adjust my other priorities to make this happen?

▲ How will I determine the success of my part in this effort?

▲ What can others expect of me?

▲ What can I expect of others?

To wrap up, here are three final thoughts on PowerSkill #4, leading. These ideas will unfailingly help you when encountering leadership challenges that threaten to shake your goals, standards, and confidence. Read them and perhaps enter them in your Journal:

1. Ralph Waldo Emerson once wrote, "Nothing great was ever achieved without enthusiasm." Leaders know that things extraordinary also never get accomplished alone.

2. Leading in relationships is a choice. By being proactive, not reactive, we can positively influence most situations. Being reactive can lead one to playing the victim. Leading is all about removing obstacles.

3. If you develop or adopt the personal leadership model, you can evaluate yourself daily by asking yourself each morning, "How will I demonstrate personal leadership today?" At the close of the day then ask, "How did I do on a scale of 1–5 in each category (attitude, behavior, and communication)?" Next, mentally average these separate scores. This daily mental gymnastic will help you develop personal leadership discipline and become detached from your ego and from the results of the day that are not within your control.

CHAPTER KEY POINTS

▲ The most effective leaders in any field are those who incorporate personal leadership qualities into their lives as a way of being.

▲ The PowerSkill of leading inspires others by tendering conditional positive regard.

▲ If you want results, practice closed-loop delegation.

▲ Effective personal leadership is really about how we manage ourselves, our projects and our relationships.

▲ Develop a mindset for thinking value and you will find that it is your key to exceptional collaborations.

▲ Focus on value exchanges in a relationship and your goals for the relationship will become clearer.

▲ Collaborative leadership is the most effective style for managing your Nifty Fifty.

▲ Appealing to the motivation for excellence sets you apart.

▲ One key to leading others well is staying as far away from role identification as possible and focusing wholly on goals.

QUESTIONS FOR YOUR POWERSKILLS JOURNAL

▲ Am I demonstrating personal leadership in my relationships on a daily basis?

▲ Am I delegating effectively (closed loop) to co-workers, clients, and people in my Nifty Fifty to achieve the results I need?

▲ Am I shaping the programs and constraints that channel energy in my team toward serving customer needs?

▲ Am I chartering and facilitating teams effectively?

PRACTICE TIPS

▲ When using the Archer Development Personal Leadership Model, how would I score myself on last week's performance on a five-point scale?

▲ Consider scoring yourself on a daily basis for thirty days and record in your PowerSkills Journal.

▲ Select three key relationships from your Nifty Fifty and do a worksheet using Ten Values/Ten Powers as a brainstorming tool. What are the items in each category that you can give and receive in these relationships beyond today's tasks or economics? Do this for the rest of your Nifty Fifty, capture your action items, and execute them. Observe improvements in the depth of your relationships.

RESOURCES

Click on **www.powerskills.com/leading** for books, videos, links and resources to develop this skill.

The Five Temptations of a CEO by Patrick Lengioni. New York: Simon & Schuster Audio, 1998. Audio Tape 04335-8

High Flyers: Developing the Next Generation of Leaders by Morgan McCall, Jr. Boston: Harvard Business School Press, 1998. ISBN 0-87584-336-0

On Becoming a Leader by Warren Bennis. Perseus Press, 1994. ISBN 0-201-409291

Principle-Centered Leadership by Stephen R. Covey. New York: Simon & Schuster, 1992. ISBN 0-671-74910-2

CHAPTER 8

POWERSKILL #5: FARMING

"We must cultivate our garden."

—Voltaire

Far from being a mundane, archaic implement of other times, the trusty agricultural plow has been vital to our human development through the ages and continues to be so today. Only by digging, hoeing, and furrowing can we be sure to earn the right (and the opportunity) to harvest what we sow.

For the first 170 million years or so in human evolution, both males and females had been hunter-gatherers, capturing animals for food and shelter and clothing, or gathering fruits, nuts, and tasty leaves and tubers to keep their families and themselves properly fed.

Somewhere around 10,000 years ago, it all changed. Some unknown innovators came up with the notion of *farming*, basically creating food (in a sense) in one's backyard rather than having to chase all over for it. By planting seeds into the ground, covering them over with dirt, then attending to them day in and day out, we could have most or all we needed. Genius. Revolutionary. It changed the world.

Actually, learning how to farm correctly was a more complicated endeavor than that, and still is—you've got to dig into the earth only so deep, sow the right number of seeds at the right distance apart, cover these up with only a precise amount of soil. You must also water not too often but not too little, you must weed and protect your innocent plants from animals and insects.

Ultimately comes harvesting mature plants and knowing how and where to store excess crops for the cold season or later consumption. At first, farming sounds so simple—until you try it! There's a lot to pay attention to and lots of planning that does not meet the eye.

Today, though few of us are agricultural specialists, cultivating and maintaining our relationship "crops" still clamor for our attention, requiring planned and careful efforts no different from those of any good farmer. In China, rice growers keep ducks or fish in rice paddies so that two foods can be harvested at the same time on the same land. Today's knowledge workers, by nurturing and cultivating the right relationships, can also learn how to work smart and multiply their gains, not merely till the soil. Learning to plan like a farmer can help us become more relationship-efficient.

Once upon a time, for example, communicating with a company's widespread constituencies could be done piecemeal, as needed, in your own way. If a company wanted to deliver certain information to its workers, management might gather them together in a company-wide meeting and tell them only what they wanted the workers to know. Then it might transmit another aspect of the same information to its investors. It could keep various segments informed about only pieces of the full picture. Rarely would such stakeholder segments overlap.

Yet today, there's the Internet and a vast array of communications channels that are fast, direct, and available to all. Communicating with your business relationships today must be more thoroughly planned and proactive, an integral component of overall business strategy. Like Chinese farmers, managers need to find ways to double and triple up on communications resources and utilization, cultivating many relationship groupings at once. The old way of just letting constituencies and customers fend for themselves while moving on to more hunting and gathering, no longer works. There's watering to be done now, weeds to pull, predators to be shooed away.

Micho Spring, president of BSMG Worldwide, one of the world's leading communications strategy consultants, explained to a leading business journal, "If you want to send a credible message to your consumers, you've got to make sure your employees believe it. Rather than just promote or get information out, most of our clients see the need to use communications proactively. The thinking is, how is this going to affect all these key elements, whether customers or employees?" Cultivating all these key segments, not ignoring them, she insists, is the only way we succeed today.

There are many resources and tools available to help us do this. Just as a tractor may be the most critical piece of farm machinery today, and one with a great many uses, one's customer/contact database may be the knowledge-worker's equivalent. Using databases equipped to make competitive information about customers and other key relationships available at the stroke of our fingertips, we can instantaneously add value to virtually every interaction we take on. Factoring in today's ubiquitous communication technologies, especially e-mail, we can also connect with anyone anywhere on the globe if we want to.

But trying to keep up with the invasive demands of information and communication systems can be perilous and exhausting, not unlike maintaining a farm or garden in the face of rapidly changing weather patterns or predicted storms. Though we have our tools readily available, the real issues center around awareness, foresight, and skill. Sometimes the sheer volume of e-mail, voice mail, meetings and videoconferences today leaves us little time to reflect and think. For this reason, *planning* for success through relationships is worth the effort. Not all relationships are important while others will make demands on us that we never expected.

Given all these considerations, we need a focused framework to make our business relationships manageable. Creating our own relationship-based farmer's almanac might be one way to help us do this. By formulating an actual plan, we can better attend to cultivating our fields of relationships.

BREAKING BAD HABITS

The 1999 Harris' Farmers Almanac advised that in December of 1999 we shouldn't neglect our *indoor* gardening chores. Clean lawnmowers, it suggested, sharpen blades, oil and polish them. Back outside we had much work to do too: clear debris out of garden beds and protect them with mulch from the cold, restake shrubs and vines, mend fence posts.

The almanac goes on to tell us that we should plant aboveground crops on the 10th, 11th, 15th and 16th and control plant pests on the first, 7th and 29th. It also includes wildlife resolutions for the new millennium as well as an aphorism for December—"Bad habits are like a comfortable bed: easy to get into but hard to get out of."

Bad habits in relationships are easy to develop too and just as costly. It's been my observation that the majority of people in business today approach their professional relationships as a sort of "just-in-time" resource, which they tap only when they actually need to. Extreme cases of this are what I call the "hit-and-run" style. Here a colleague only calls you when he needs something and then, after receiving it, never even acknowledges your contribution.

What's really amusing about all this is the language hit-and-runners use, often very telling: "I need to pick your brain" all the while not really listening, not giving back. Or "I want to bounce something off you" but they never have time for you to bounce anything off of them! Failure to reciprocate or consistently communicate unfortunately represents the norm, not the exception in this busy professional world. It's usually not intentional but rather the result of an imbalance of focus. True business leaders take care to balance relationship management with task management even though tasks are more concrete and easier to focus on. They understand well that everyone, whether they recognize it or not, possesses personal currencies.

CREATING YOUR CURRENCY

We traditionally define currency as money in some form, but *currency* actually represents value in a broader sense. A wise person's counsel, a letter of commendation, a web site recommendation, a personal gift of appreciation are also currencies. Sharing additional knowledge by-products of our work with clients and colleagues can also provide a currency above and beyond the expected.

Each one of us has a uniqueness, often in the form of personal interests like music, literature, sports, education, child development, or fitness that at times becomes a common denominator in bonding with others. Taking it one step further with a sincere initiative to follow-through and to surprise or delight another person with some form of personal currency can transform a relationship. It says you care. Done with finesse and without fanfare, sharing your currencies to reinforce desired behaviors (i.e., rewarding contributions to a project, recognizing valuable referrals) can create exceptional good will.

Years ago, an executive I regarded highly started his own business and consulted with me about his go-to-market strategy. I enjoyed the creative session with him and followed up to give him some specific leads after "talking it up" with a few of my own clients. One night, weeks later, I came home from work surprised to find a carton of red wine with a thank you note for helping him win his first client. For me and him, vintage dry red wines are a currency, and he knew this. I never forgot his generosity. Since he lived 60 miles away, I was even more impressed because I had no expectations other than a verbal thank you, if that. This kindness really set him apart in my mind. Developing your personal currencies is a way to bring who you are into your work and relationships. From your profiling of your VIRs you will find people who share your culinary, travel, and other tips that, when appropriate, can be shared. Sometimes a currency might be a particularly well told humorous story, but not all of us are naturals at that one.

In theatre we recall that there are "flat characters" and "round characters." It is the round character that we remember and the generous ones that we cherish. Using your personal currencies in reinforcing relationships is an area of considerable creativity that will never be covered in a policy manual but it can build depth in your relationships.

AN ON-GOING PROCESS

A "connection behavior" I employ regularly is one I use while on vacation: before I go away, I print out my address book, then hoist it out one day while I'm basking by a pool or lolling at a café. There I hand-write a number of postcards, no long, drawn-out message, just a brief message like, "Terrific time, your kids would love it here!" Then I address it, stamp it, and it's done! The whole project might take twenty or thirty minutes tops, depending on how many I do, and yet the goodwill I create in resolidified bonds, is immense. I have fun doing it, too, sitting there as I do in a straw hat in the sun, simultaneously proving that PowerSkill #5, farming, unlike more traditional agriculture, does not need to be back-breaking, sweaty toil for one instant.

You too can incorporate similar farming techniques into your work week or work month or work year. This will build you a relationship-management framework that's ongoing. Enter key events for your Nifty Fifty relationships into your calendar and seek other ways to utilize vacations, business trips, commutes, or other "nonproductive" blocks of time for your farming activities.

It's a good idea in fact to connect "live" with your VIRs a minimum of five or six times per year, with at least two of those touches, ideally, face-to-face. Alan Weiss, in his superb book, *Million Dollar Consulting*, suggests that, "If you haven't spoken to a client in at least six months, you're not staying in enough contact." You probably want to do much better than that, never going longer than two months making some kind of contact with each client. Weiss would likely agree with me because later in his book he adds, "You can never communicate *too much* with a client."

STAYING IN TOUCH

There are many types of "touches" you can make to create a good stay-in-touch (SIT) program, including regular mail, e-mail, telephone, fax, conference call, voice mail, and, last but not least, good old-fashioned but increasingly powerful...face-to-face! A mixture of all of these will afford you an effective SIT.

One of the best SIT corporate programs I've ever heard of is the one required of its financial planners by American Express Financial Services. AMEX planners are expected to communicate with their clients regularly throughout each year—at least six times by mail, four by phone, at least once in person. This continuous dialogue re-introduces clients to their planner's value and inspires them to jointly investigate new investment opportunities. Such a farm system breeds trusting relationships between planners and clients who become re-acquainted with their planner's sincere interests in their financial well being.

To emulate the American Express model, you want to consider your *dialogue mix.* The many ways you can communicate with a contact, while keeping in mind his/her dialogue preferences. Amex primarily uses regular mail, phone calling, and face-to-face. Basics all, but nowadays there are a lot more to draw upon than those. Many nonprofit associations, for example, stay in touch with their members by adding faxes to their dialogue mix, usually for announcements of upcoming events, and/or emails, for announcements, surveys, information-sharing, problem-solving, decision-making.

THE DIALOGUE MIX

Whatever you use, you do want to be sure that whomever you're communicating with desires the touch modality you choose. Marketing professionals, for example, understand that all editors and reporters are different in their attitudes toward communications vehicles. Some prefer e-mail, some like communication by fax; some prefer snail-mail, some the phone. If you're seeking press coverage, then, you don't want to just slap an e-mail list together and treat all your media targets the same, just because it may be more convenient for *you.* You must tailor each touch modality to appeal to the individual you're attempting to reach.

There are many touch modalities now available to us. Undoubtedly, more are coming our way that, at this writing, none of us know about. For now, consider the following partially completed Dialogue Mix shown in Exhibit 8.1. How are you using these modalities of communication and how often?

> **EXHIBIT 8.1 Dialogue Mix—Key Client Example**

MODALITY	FREQUENCY
Face-to-face	2 x /year
Letter	3 x /year
Newsletter	Quarterly
Phone	>1 x /month
Survey participation	1 x /year
Toll-free numbers	
Handwritten note	
Voice mail	
Fax	
Pager	
Company bulletin board	
Electronic bulletin board	
E-mail	
Extranet	
Cell phone	
Video Conferencing	
Website	

Like American Express, you also must consider frequency. How often you communicate with your contacts will have either a positive or a negative impact on your relationship. Do you talk daily? When working very closely on a project, even multiple times per day may not be unreasonable.

Do you communicate weekly? This could be the right pacing to keep a client updated on your progress or to keep your boss aware of your needs.

How about monthly or quarterly? This may be the right timing to keep in touch between engagements.

How about e-mail? Do you periodically send an e-mail notice out to all of your contacts, just to advise them of a recent development of yours or to pass along some new knowledge?

Even before e-mail came along, which has made communication so easy that none of us any longer has an excuse, many great business leaders already had their framework intact. Sending out newsletters, article reprints, announcements of new products, or of new additions to staff are standard in many industries. Or perhaps keeping contact via frequent telephone calls or by committing to visit your customers each and every week (like Snap-On Tools) is more your style.

Some companies are now mailing out Thanksgiving cards every year to their customers and friends. In this way, holiday greetings are out before the seasonal rush and at the same time expresses appreciation to everyone for their support of the past year and for their future support the year to come.

Whatever system you use, some kind of regular Stay-in-Touch model will reinforce top-of-mind awareness. Is monthly farming using a newsletter or product update card appropriate for *your* business? How about the American Express model—six mailings per year, four phone contacts, one face-to-face? Try a few things out, test them, evaluate. Sooner or later you will choose the dialogue mix that works for you and your VIRs.

You may, in fact, be surprised at how little time or effort it all takes—minutes a day when you break it down over the course of a year, an hour here, twenty minutes here. Perhaps your farming today includes only a luncheon or breakfast meeting. As long as it's systematic, you'll soon be remembering your VIRs effortlessly, continuing your dialogue with them over the phone, meetings, meals, by fax, or e-mail, and transforming the whole process into one both painless and smooth.

NEMAWASHI

Nemawashi is a term Japanese business people use to describe a technique for reducing misunderstanding and gaining agreement from everyone in advance. It is frequently used during times of negotiation and major decision-making. Interestingly, the original meaning of this word is "to dig around the roots of a tree" in order to make the tree easier to move.

Best used, its practitioners say, when people of differing opinions need time to adjust those opinions, *nemawashi* employs principles akin to tree-moving, such as the notion of "digging around the roots." Try moving a tree without first digging around and loosening the roots and you'll have a whale of a hard time. Dig up the roots first, however, the most massive tree will come out with ease. *Nemawashi* is just like that: with the approach of an impending decision, lobbying or educating everyone involved, one-to-one, adjusts opinions and builds support before the formal group work begins. The decision you want (i.e., the tree you wish to move) follows in kind.

The Japanese have honed this farming PowerSkill, *nemawashi*, as a process of establishing and growing relationships over a long period of time, to an art. They have applied this concept to opening doors into new markets with long-term gain in mind, not quick profits. The bigger focus is the building of trust in order to gain productive understanding of a new market.

With the emphasis on self-directed work teams today, developing a consensus like this before formal decision-making is a smart approach. As more and more decisions get made by committees, practicing nemawashi lays the groundwork for building team-wide support for your course of action. The practice of nemawashi plants seeds or ideas with your VIRs and moves ideas, projects, or proposals through today's labyrinthine organizations. A variation of the concept of "power of suggestion," *nemawashi* can become a key farming implement nestled in your PowerSkills tool shed.

PLANTING SEEDS: THE ASTONISHING POWER OF SUGGESTION

We've all heard the phrase, "the power of suggestion." We take for granted that this cliché has much validity or impact. We all know that it does, it works so well whenever we try it. For that reason, it's always been hard for me to understand why it is generally overlooked when professionals seek to manage their professional relations. Great ideas and great initiatives, after all, do not suddenly burst out of nowhere with no help from man, beast, nor God. The best ideas tend to evolve after much iteration among a diverse set of creative people spending lots of time questioning and adding value to the initial notion. Only after ideas are fully developed in this manner will the selling of those ideas proceed relatively smoothly.

When we plant the right seeds in the right minds in the right way, we guide a process in which others have time to invest in our idea's success. Without proceeding in this manner, overcoming resistance to change will not really be possible. But once we've laid the groundwork for change, we may then move along to watching our ideas flower and harvesting them when the time is right.

INVESTORS, HUNTERS, AND FARMERS

Why do people come to investors?

Sure, they come for the money, because a bank has turned them down, or they know going in that no bank would even consider lending them funds to start a "risky" venture. Or maybe they need more money than any traditional bank would be willing to commit.

But people also come to investors to tap into an investor's networks and for feedback and advice. Over the past five years I have become involved with an investment group called Walnut Venture Associates, based outside of Boston. Comprised of former CEOs and high-tech executives, our meetings are energizing, challenging, and filled with wit as investment proposals are reviewed. Around the table is a cadre of individuals with professional success stories, hunters by and large who have come now to a sporting phase of their careers and fully appreciate the concept of nurturing new enterprise "seeds" into proud saplings and eventually trees.

The funny thing is that after a while most of the best deals come to our group without any hunting on our part at all. While each of my co-investors have been successful hunters throughout their careers, farming more than hunting now predominates in each of our lives. Managing relationships and financial assets by watering, weeding, and treating the soil (translation: qualifying a deal, suggesting strategic adjustments, testing the concepts, introducing management and business partners, infusing blocks of capital), allows a new enterprise to take off, not just marginally but at ten, twenty times its original investment.

The paradox of farming, then, is that, once you've done your hunting and initial planting in earlier days, your hard work will be eventually rewarded in satisfiable and perhaps unexpected ways.

Stephen Covey called this "the law of the farm." Give things time to grow, and the time they must have, he says, and you will reap the benefits down the line when your yield is ready.

PUT YOUR PRODUCERS ON THE LINE

Some of us can still enjoy going to a farm stand where you can actually buy native-grown produce directly from the farmer or choose a pick-your-own option and for a few minutes become a hard-working farmer yourself. Though we always have the option today of buying our strawberries, corn, squash, or beans at the nearest supermarket superstore, even at a lower price perhaps, we can nonetheless still savor the experience of shopping at a farm stand. We enjoy the smell, the look, the feel of being right there in the middle of it all, fields all around, tractor sitting idly 50 yards away.

Going to the source frequently matters. As customers we like to be proximate, at least occasionally, and interact with developers of a product or a service. How else to explain Saturn car owners taking an annual jaunt to the Saturn factory jamboree? Or Jeep owners doing the same at the top of some mountain?

Why else would owners of Macintosh computers journey to New York or San Francisco for Apple's yearly MacWorld convention? Why else would baseball fans schedule winter vacations in Florida or Arizona to be close to their favorite team's spring training?

If only your sales staff interacts with customers and clients during the sales process, significant opportunities for customer intimacy and bonding will be missed. Why not get everyone involved? Of course, your sales manager might want to help devise a "customer interaction event" such as those at Saturn or Jeep, perhaps coaching nonsales staff to actually interact in a sales-oriented way. Finding creative ways to bring your firm's expertise to the customer can yield bountiful rewards.

EXAMPLE: Whenever Staples opens a new store, it invites new customers in for a free business-marketing seminar. The assumption is that if Staples can help its entrepreneurial customers become better at their own business development activities, they will be highly successful at they do and keep contributing to Staples sales for many years to come. No overt sales tactics are employed during these seminars, just a competent knowledgeable marketing expert (not a Staples employee) and Staples staff in the wings to assist and answer questions. Attendees, as a result, fill up shopping carts when a seminar is over and line up at the store's cash registers, knowing they will return again when new supplies, office furniture or an office appliance is needed in the future.

CLIENT RELATIONSHIP MANAGEMENT AND THE SALES CYCLE

Companies typically train their sales people in a too-narrow fashion by teaching them to manage accounts guided by the "sales cycle." The focus here is on separating customers from their money, though with a veneer of human relations understanding. The reality, however, is that what's traditionally been called the sales cycle is actually a subset of a broader relationship cycle. The effective client relationship management cycle involves six key phases: creating top-of-mind awareness; analyzing needs and requirements; testing solutions; developing proposals and contracting; deploying the solution and maintaining communication through a stay-in-touch program. All too often, the sales professional is expected to skip everything but the presentation, budget discussion and closing activities contained in the proposal and contracting phase. The focus on the bigger picture, ironically, will actually shorten the sales cycle!

Have you ever found yourself stunned and amazed to learn that an entrepreneur in a tiny, unknown company has all of a sudden landed several major accounts in your space with big, well-known corporations? Upon closer examination, even more astonishing, the coup may have taken place within a matter of three or four weeks. Meanwhile, your sales directors are bemoaning the length of the sales cycle.

Upon even closer inspection, we often find that the entrepreneur has been cultivating those relationships for years. It was not, in fact, some "lucky break" that struck unexpectedly. The seeds had been planted long ago.

This, in fact, is how the most successful business leaders shorten their sales cycles. By spending literally lifetimes hunting, and building, and farming their relationships, great business leaders position themselves for opportunities that their competitors must suddenly, and frantically, ramp up for.

Conversely, tragically, the vast majority of sales training programs do little to teach, encourage, or reward salespeople to build long-term relationships into the sales process. No wonder that 20% of most sales forces generate 80% of the sales.

In working with and researching sales organizations for 25 years, I have discovered a clear parallel between professionals who understand and employ all five PowerSkills—positioning, hunting, coaching, leading, and farming—and an ability to deliver desired or unanticipated results to clients old and new.

Use of PowerSkills also enables one to quickly demonstrate potential results to prospects. Business leaders who have learned to incorporate the building of the "right" relationships into their sales cycles give less credence to how long a sales cycle is supposed to be. After all, relationship building, in their minds, never ends. The abstract concept of a sales cycle needs to be supported by the Relationship Equation of establishing trust, value, and dialogue.

EXPECTATION ENGINEERING

Building trust in relationships is about setting, meeting, and exceeding expectations. It's also about making and keeping promises. When we promise value and fail to deliver without at least some alternative or honest resetting of expectations, we have put ourselves perhaps irretrievably on the fast track to destroying all trust in a particular relationship.

When we exceed expectations, however, it's a different story. Toyota remains in the top five among worldwide automobile sellers, for example, because its corporate culture supports expectation engineering. Toyota customer survey systems act like ongoing consumer investigations, noting what its customers like, don't like, and "wish" they could have. As a result, Toyota product developments frequently anticipate what customers might want without even being specifically asked or told, introducing fresh ideas for more vehicle models, lighter-weight materials, and faster cruising speeds.

"These kinds of companies ask totally different questions," says Jack Ricchiuto, a Cleveland-based creativity consultant and author of

Collaborative Creativity: Unleashing the Power of Shared Thinking (Oak Hill Press, 1997). "A traditional set of management questions begins with 'How can we listen to our market better?' and 'How can we meet customers' requirements?' But creative companies like Toyota ask, 'How can we *surprise* our market?' Answering that one requires an ultra-high degree of commitment to management creativity." Innovation and farming go hand in hand.

OBSERVE THE CUSTOMER-VALUE HIERARCHY

Frustrated that your business relies primarily on new business? Wondering what you can do to keep customers coming back, as well as increase each customer's *level* of business?

If you want to reap the profitable rewards of repeat customers and systematically increase each customer's buying activity, then pay attention to your "customer-value hierarchy." Karl Albrecht, author of *Service America* and *The Only Thing that Matters* has provided some excellent frameworks for understanding this term, which is meant to describe how to deliver *exceptional* customer value through total service quality.

We can provide, Albrecht maintains, at least four levels of customer value:

1. Basic
2. Expected
3. Desired
4. Unanticipated

Some companies like Toyota hit Level #4 each and every time.

FARMERS KNOW WHEN TO GIVE THANKS

One of the most underexploited principles in the business to business world is the power of recognition and reward systems. Though attention is indeed paid to this area, too much energy tends to be placed upon untimely compensation and incentive systems that improperly direct behavior. To properly build and enhance relationships, however, timely and specific recognition and other meaningful personalized rewards cannot be forgotten.

We all know this yet fail to implement it in our daily lives. We say, for example, we enjoy the pleasure of giving but we then run out and get so consumed with our own agendas we usually forget to do so. Simple thank you's often get put off until "later," which more often than not becomes "never."

One solution is to maintain your journal and make it a point to enter your need to thank someone tomorrow or pick up a nice gift or other reward. You might also vigilantly manage your VIRs with a calendar program, as we spoke about earlier. Whatever technique you use, the best relationship farmers make recognizing others a way of life, nurturing their relationship gardens regularly.

FARMERS KNOW WHEN TO HARVEST

Traditional farmers understand the principle of timing in running their operation. They learn from mentors and coaches (usually their parents, farmers before them) how to do this, or from hard-bitten experience (from losses due to droughts, insect invasions, floods). It's an important lesson because timing tells them when to actually pick their crops, to harvest, and when to leave them alone.

In business, timing also helps signal us when to harvest our goods. The best time, for example, to engage a customer in your marketing program would be immediately following a successful engagement, when your customer's satisfaction is at its peak. Exceed your VIRs' expectations and they will always be pleased to return the favor by drawing you up a letter of endorsement or passing your name along to new prospects.

Ralph Waldo Emerson once said, "Every act rewards itself." With farms all around him in little Concord, Massachusetts in those days, he certainly knew what he was talking about. By simply investing in relationships, coaching, giving value, and saying thanks, we reap a harvest for ourselves initially impossible to predict.

CALCULATING THE YIELDS

Farmers know relevant vital statistics on ratios of feeds to yields. They know how much they need to inject into their systems (seed, animal feed) in order to produce X amounts of a specific crop or animals that will weigh Y. In this way, they can fairly accurately calculate costs and profits.

It's always been amazing to me that highly intelligent teams of professionals rarely employ similar methods. Though working within the same company, serving the same customers, they nonetheless operate with little or no synergy and at high levels of misunderstanding, conflict and inefficiency.

By attention to our VIR databases, we can learn how to calculate such yields for ourselves. Trial and error is a part of it; systematically recording what happens and trying again, or attempting a new strategy, will serve us well too.

Your company undoubtedly has some kind of a customer database. You also undoubtedly use some kind of paper or computer-based Rolodex to track your own customers and contacts. Yet it is still the exceptional company that maintains up-to-date information about customers, incorporating your information, that of your colleagues and peers and in general any details other than mere purchase history. As a result, your most highly calibrated VIR relationships get mixed in with the broadest categories of "contacts" and are all but forgotten. Tremendous leverage is lost in most organizations for this simple fact.

Companies spend millions attempting to address their customer-information-file problems with sophisticated sales and marketing automation software (known as CRM-Customer Relationship Management software). In Chapter 10, we will explore these and other relationship tools as resources to supplement your PowerSkills activities. They offer a significant sophisticated adjunct in the effort to become truly customer-intimate.

Yet the problem for most companies is that to become customer-intimate on a high level they need three things overall: strategies, systems, and behaviors (culture). Whether a multi-million-dollar CRM software package for a company or a one hundred-dollar contact management database for an individual, such computer tools will prove worthless if the user does not develop PowerSkills behaviors to also manage their relationships. On the other hand, great strategies and relationship behaviors without a software system to implement them will shortchange your PowerSkills effectiveness as well.

Some day not too far in the future, I would hope that many, if not most, of the top business leaders will be regularly employing these best practices of relationship management in some form or another. Should this day come they will probably also be utilizing software and reward systems to enhance them in order to align their relationship-management practices with focused business strategies. This potent combination will produce spectacular, unanticipated results for their employees, investors, customers, partners, and the community. But the cultural and behavioral piece will always yield the biggest payoff of the lot, and employing a PowerSkills framework will also contribute an ability to measure the entire effort as well.

EARLY HARVEST: INITIATING
A BREAKTHROUGH VIR PROJECT

A word of caution: Developing a detailed customer information file system (CIF) can be time-consuming and costly. Although it may be an important strategic component for your business development system in the long run, in the shorter run it could become a goal in itself and derail your ramp time progress. A shortcut for you and your team instead might be to try pushing Mother Nature to grant you an early harvest by setting your sights on a "breakthrough" project.

A breakthrough project exhibits the following characteristics: It has an immediate business benefit, is achievable within a short time frame (using only available resources), and it creates momentum for a strategic initiative. Here's one method I advocate frequently to my clients:

▲ Create a common file structure for your Nifty Fifty.

▲ Enter into a simple database.

▲ Aggregate the Nifty Fifty contacts from each of your top people.

▲ Develop a VIR communications program for key individuals and groups.

You will now have created the beginnings of a very powerful VIR database that you can use for developing top-of-mind communication programs such as planning events, making special offers, and following up with your stay-in-touch programs.

Just getting yourself and your organization to begin thinking about the who, what, when, where, why, and how of developing and cultivating powerful business relationships delivers immediate benefits like information flow, improved collaboration, market knowledge, and deal flow. Applying PowerSkills principles to these relationships makes action steps your organization (and you personally) should be taking next, clearer. By thinking through the groupings of your VIRs it will be easier to see where gaps in relationships lie and which groupings require additional recruitment. This means planting new seeds, going out hunting again if necessary, re-evaluating your positioning, coaching neglected VIRs, and, of course, increasing your levels of leading and farming.

In the final section of this book, we will also examine how to take your developing PowerSkills one stage further, right into the heart of your organization or team, leveraging them in your work with your peers and colleagues. We'll also review some "powertools"—customer database software programs and other technological aids that can multiply your PowerSkills practices.

By integrating PowerSkills firmly within the context of everyday business life, we make them more powerful then ever. Since working in teams and resourcing high-tech tools fit the very definition of current business life, these cannot be ignored if we are to attain maximum professional and personal effectiveness. Master these areas and you will undoubtedly achieve success where it counts the most: in your business's bottom-line.

CHAPTER KEY POINTS

▲ Learning to plan and manage relationship assets like farmers can help us leverage established relationships.

▲ The old way of letting constituencies and customers fend for themselves no longer works. Now, to keep your customers coming back, there's watering to be done, weeds to pull, predators to be shooed away.

▲ Not all relationships are important. Therefore *planning* for success through key relationships is worth the effort.

▲ True business leaders balance relationship management with task management, understanding that everyone carries a personal currency.

▲ Connect with your VIRs a minimum of five or six times per year, at least two of those touches, ideally, face-to-face.

▲ As customers we like to be proximate or have access to the developers and creators of a product or a service.

▲ If only your sales staff interacts with customers, significant opportunities for customer intimacy will be missed.

▲ Focusing on the bigger picture (the relationship cycle) will shorten the sales cycle!

▲ Building trust in relationships is about setting, meeting, and exceeding expectations. It's also about making and keeping promises.

▲ Farming is not mere maintenance—innovation and farming go hand in hand.

▲ To properly build and enhance relationships, timely and specific recognition, and other meaningful personalized rewards, cannot be forgotten.

▲ In business, timing is critical to harvest our value.

▲ Great relationship behaviors without the software to support them shortchanges PowerSkills effectiveness.

QUESTIONS FOR YOUR POWERSKILLS JOURNAL

▲ Do I follow up diligently on action items after meetings or discussions?

▲ Have I maintained the integrity and quality of my database of clients and colleagues?

▲ Once I have "sold" or completed a project do I stay engaged with that client through the life cycle of the engagement and beyond?

▲ Have I developed a stay-in-touch program with my Nifty Fifty and mapped out periodic reviews, events, and communications on an annual calendar to track results?

▲ Should I adjust the modalities and frequency of communications (the dialogue mix) with my constituents?

▲ Am I capturing, utilizing, and sharing the knowledge by-products of my work with clients and influencers?

▲ What am I really doing in the course of my daily work to proactively establish long-term, win-win relationships?

▲ Am I leveraging my Nifty Fifty with a referral strategy or collaborative exchanges?

▲ Have I analyzed my client contact points (appearance, business card, web site, voice and e-mail messages, reception, correspondence) to bolster the quality of interactions?

▲ Should I be pruning my contact or Nifty Fifty list to invest energy in the right places?

▲ Am I producing value that is beyond the expected?

▲ Has our organization become easy to do business with? If not, what can I do to change this?

PRACTICE TIPS

Informally interview some of your customers and Nifty Fifty role models that you believe have a strong customer relationship-management system or approach and share some lessons learned about cultivating partner-like relationships.

RESOURCES

Click on **www.powerskills.com/farming** for reference guides, readings, links and resources to develop this skill. You will also find links to sites that provide information about technologies to implement customer relationship management, loyalty, and stay-in-touch programs.

After-Marketing: How to Keep Customers for Life Through Relationship Marketing by Terry G. Vavra. Burr Ridge, Ill: Irwin Professional Publishing, 1992. ISBN 0-78630405-7

The One to One Future: Building Relationships One Customer at a Time by Don Peppers and Martha Rogers, Ph.D. Currency Doubleday: 1993. ISBN 0-385-485662

The Only Thing That Matters: Bringing the Power of the Customer into the Center of Your Business by Karl Albrecht. New York, NY: HarperBusiness, 1992. ISBN 0-88730-639-X

PART 3

POWERSKILLS AND THE HIGH PERFORMANCE ORGANIZATION

CHAPTER 9

POWERSKILLS AND THE SELF-ALIGNING ORGANIZATION

"Leaders must somehow align the decisions and behaviors of managers and workers to deliver value to customers faster and better than the competition"

—Jon R. Katzenbach,

Teams at the Top

Seems like it's been around forever, long before the start of any of our lives, and it's such an institution that, unless you're actively involved with it, you may not even notice its building as you hurry past on a busy city street. If an ad for it came on your TV you might even tune it out. Yet somewhere in the recesses of your mind you figure it must be doing something right/something good because it's always been there. But for many of us, it's hard to articulate exactly what it does.

What am I hinting at? What organization is easily missed, or dismissed, yet serves 16 million Americans each year (8 million of them children)? Located in 10,000 U.S. communities alone, in all fifty states and 130 countries—57,000 volunteers in the U.S. alone—

it does great social good, partners with social service agencies, and contributes mightily to healthy living and spiritual lifestyles.

It's spawned three universities, has directly assisted our Armed Forces in time of war, and even gets credit for the invention of two sports, volleyball and basketball, and coining of the term "body-building." Know what I'm referring to by now? Still not sure? Want to give up?

Then here's the answer: It's the YMCA, subject of a popular, campy disco song in the late 70s, but in reality an international alliance that's been in our midst since the first Y opened in England in 1844 and the first American Y began in Boston in 1850.

What's so great about the YMCA? What specific services does it actually offer beyond its popular image of inexpensive rooms for men, a few workout facilities and gyms here and there, and community meeting spaces? Most important, why on earth would I begin a chapter on self-aligning organizations with a description of it?

It may surprise you to learn that our old friend and neighbor the YMCA may in fact embody a stirring example of a powerful, effective *self-aligning organization*. Throughout a full century and a half of history, it's risen repeatedly to the task of fulfilling its core values and evolving mission by utilizing PowerSkills-like methodologies. In the process, it's achieved a steadfastly loyal, generations-old customer base and continually renewing value to the community. In a fashion, YMCAs have been coaching and providing leadership training for decades.

Although begun by evangelicals, its "target market" from the start embraced persons of all creeds, backgrounds, races, and persuasions, crossing rigid class and religious lines at a time when churches in particular had been insisting such segments of the population stay apart. Its mission arose in response to terrible, unhealthy social conditions in industrial era England (open sewers, thugs and pickpockets, black soot spoiling the air, garbage in the streets) and has since endeavored to eradicate or at least ease them for the good of everyone.

Despite historical disruptions of tremendous magnitude (the Civil War, two world wars, the Great Depression, upheavals of the 1960s), the Y has held to its mission to the present day. Though precise expression of core values may have shifted here and there, these values have remained basically the same throughout decades as well. Consider: "The improvement of the spiritual, mental, social and physical condition of men" (1866); a commitment to "spirit, mind and body" (1890); uniting young men to "maintain their physical and mental vigor and ...usefulness and service to themselves and the community" (1932); an emphasis on families (late 1940s), on healthy lifestyles (1970s); character development in the form of "caring, honesty, respect and responsibility" (1990s). Through it all, YMCAs have somehow remained true to their original strategic intent: to build "strong kids, strong families and strong communities."

But in terms of alignment, it's the way the Y as a vast and far-flung organization that has achieved this may be most instructive of all. Y's have always encouraged organization-wide self-examination; for one thing, its managers are committed to functioning day-to-day as though leadership was a bottom-up, middle-out affair. Also Y directors try not to "boss" or play command-and-control. Coaching both employees and volunteers to stay on mission, and to keep volunteers on mission, is the YMCA's norm.

In turn, most staffers see themselves as direct fulfillers of the big picture, passionately dedicated to "customer" results. By whatever manner Y core values were articulated through the ages, they served to attract workers to Y service. Employment at a YMCA can never be like "just a job," Y employees say, insisting their contributions must make a difference for those they serve, and a visible one at that.

Organizational attributes such as these, you'll learn later in this chapter, make up the heart and soul of what I have labeled the self-aligning organization (SAO). Because of its core values and an impressive organizational structure founded on vibrant human networks, the YMCAs of the world combine and largely convey all the "right stuff." Sadly, we cannot say the same for the majority of for-profit companies.

Up until this chapter, we have spoken of PowerSkills primarily as tools you can use to make your professional life more effective, empowered, and energized. Develop and apply the five PowerSkills to vitalize your relationships, we have said, and you'll surely end up with the bottom-line results you desire.

As a business leader, you naturally wish to be involved in a high performing, customer-focused organization, in other words—a winning team. That always proves a lot more fun and satisfying than waging battle after losing battle on things that don't matter. Who wants to spend a working life year in and year out as a round peg in a politics-fraught, resource-draining square hole? That's why we'll examine in this chapter the other side of the coin, the "excellent" organization, enterprise rich in PowerSkills and dedicated to serving its customers without reserve.

ALIGNMENT IS KEY

Perhaps the most critical aspect in creating such a high performance, customer-centric organization is *alignment*. Why is alignment so important? Many business analysts and writers have studied this dynamic recently and have come up with specific theories. George Labovitz and Victor Rosansky, authors of The *Power of Alignment*, have done some of the best conceptual work in this area.

In their book, these two management experts advance a model of alignment and convincingly illustrate how aligned organizations (Federal Express, for example) typically function more productively than nonaligned. Defining alignment as "linking people, processes, customers, business strategies and leadership," Labovitz and Rosansky describe vertical alignment as connecting strategy with people, and horizontal alignment as connecting processes with customers. At Federal Express, drivers, managers, customer-service reps all see the swift and safe delivery of packages as impacting the people they service. There is no disconnect there. Cultivate such mindsets, they insist, and success cannot be avoided.

Phrasing this another way, we might recall the words of Lou Gerstner: "The last thing IBM needs right now is a new strategy." He had meant that the formulation of strategy and proposing of systems is typically the easy part. But creating true cultures that fall in step with either strategy or systems (or both)—not so easy! Once again, Lou Gerstner had the right idea.

EXAMPLE: Besides the story of the YMCA that opened this chapter, there are many other striking illustrations of self-aligning organizations spurring the kind of employee spirit that, by linking people with processes and strategy, drives continuous improvement and customer satisfaction. Alignment can make an organization unbeatable.

Consider the fast rise of Ben and Jerry's Ice Cream from obscure, small-time Vermont ice cream shop to national institution. Whether you partake of Ben and Jerry's products or not, you've undoubtedly heard about them. Likely too, you possess at least a vague recollection of what both founders, Ben and Jerry, look like.

Though some of the credit for this goes to the ice cream giant's marketing division—you see both owners' images whenever you pick up a pint of their product—much also goes to the reputation Ben and Jerry themselves have developed as caring, listening, responsive (i.e., alignment-oriented) top executives. Many tourists in Vermont put a visit to their factory on the same sightseeing itinerary that includes excursions to the Green Mountain state's lakes, ski slopes, covered bridges, and fall foliage. Tours of Ben and Jerry's attract people who love their ice cream, can take it or leave it, have never even tried it. Of course, converts are made every day from free samples available on each tour of Cherry Garcia or Chunky Monkey.

But a tour of Ben and Jerry's is more than just a look at a few ice cream machines and a taste of its product. The tour includes a fun video about how the company got started, how it produces its product, and how it treats employees. In the video you see smiling faces of workers at company picnics, on the job and engaged in creative problem-solving. Then, as you tour, you encounter these same high-energy employees in their work habitats—bustling about in bright yellow jumpsuits, working together in teams, nodding hello to tourists as they pass them in the hallways, and laughing with co-workers.

Structures in place explain much of this. It's a company heavy on participation, coaching, listening skills, open communication, and flexible attitudes. Every worker belongs to a process team engaged in ongoing dialogues about how to improve things, both internally and out in the marketplace. Rewards are given for wacky, out-of-the-box ideas, even ones that may never be adopted. What should be a factory full of boring, monotonous, low-skilled job slots instead pulsates with vitality, commitment, humor, ideas, interplay. There's even a process team devoted to fun in the workplace, which Jerry himself has taken to overseeing in an official capacity.

And as if all this weren't enough, working at Ben and Jerry's includes an employee benefit not found in any other corporation anywhere in the world. Every Friday, workers can select two free quarts of ice cream to take home with them! That's alignment for you, the Ben and Jerry's way!

GETTING IN WHACK: ACHIEVING ALIGNMENT

In studying the challenges of developing the potential of both teams and individual leaders in today's business world, Jon R. Katzenbach, author of *Teams at the Top*, has defined four primary elements that leaders can use to align decisions and actions of their people:

▲ Formal structures—as represented in the organization chart

- ▲ Management processes—work or action flows that cut across the organization
- ▲ Forums—councils, committees, small work groups
- ▲ Informal networks

The last, Katzenbach points out, is the most neglected element of the four. While most organizations spend untold energies on the first three, few have developed sophisticated systems for harnessing the fourth.

Of course this comes as no surprise to the devotee and practitioner of PowerSkills. The greatest business leaders know that alignment in organizations without PowerSkills is virtually impossible. Since an organization's informal human network serves as the prime cultural mover of alignment, only by employing PowerSkills can we catalyze this mover, particularly when aided by what I call tribal instincts.

What do I mean by *tribal instincts?* We now understand the need for alignment, but can alignment principles be distributed in a practical way? Too many analysts leave this question hanging. By educating a workforce to PowerSkills, an organization can resolve this issue and get alignment up and operating. The use of PowerSkills infuses a workforce with tribal instincts that naturally focus energies and attitudes of individuals and teams in the right directions. To be specific, I see "tribal instinct" as a synonym for culture, which is defined as "an established way of doing things." Get your organization doing the right things (building profitable relationships) again and again and again and you will surely thrive.

Imagine, if you will, an organization acting on the credo, shown in Exhibit 9.1.

> ### EXHIBIT 9.1 The PowerSkills Credo

> ▶ We will **position** our added value and establish credibility with and in the minds of those who matter.

> ▶ We will **hunt** for the people with ideas and information that can benefit and add to our vision and help our customers.

> ▶ We will **coach** and build learning relationships as we deliver and exchange great value in our daily work.

> ▶ We will **lead** our partners, prospects and clients to victory with our innovations.

> ▶ We will **farm** the communities of interest that we create for long-term mutual benefit.

What would you think of an organization that focused its energies in these ways? Unstoppable! To paraphrase the now well-known mantra from the movie *Field of Dreams:* If you build profitable relationships, based on your company's core competencies and values, they (i.e., droves of customers) will come!

ATTRIBUTES OF A SELF-ALIGNING ORGANIZATION

By boiling down the experiences of the over 10,000 business leaders I have interviewed, and building on the contributions of authors such as Labovitz, Rosansky, Katzenbach, and Wiersema among many others, I have synthesized the common denominators into the following top ten attributes of self-aligning organizations.

1. **HAS LEADERS THAT FUNCTION LIKE COACHES**—Leaders in a truly self-aligning organization do not bark orders, get angry, throw fits. They coach their people, provide resources, and ask how people are doing. Daily, they exhibit the PowerSkill of coaching, fostering a coaching culture that empowers everyone and drives continuous improvement.

2. **HAS CLEARLY ARTICULATED CORE VALUES**—In the self-aligning organization, everyone knows what they stand for, and what their organization stands for. Customers are served with common core values in mind, and workers serve each other guided by the same.

3. **STAYS FOCUSED ON MISSION**—Because the self-aligning organization's mission is clearly articulated and often repeated, its informal human networks keep its mission alive. As in the case of core values (#2), this attribute provides each individual worker a guideline for moment-to-moment decisions.

4. **DEDICATES ITSELF TOTALLY TO CUSTOMER RESULTS**—Everyone in the SAO knows his/her raison d'être: satisfying the customer, whether customer means client, purchaser, colleague, business partner, boss, or supplier. Everyone in the SAO is seen as a customer and everyone gets treated like one.

5. **LEVERAGES CORE COMPETENCIES (THROUGH STRATEGIC RELATIONSHIPS)**—The self-aligning organization knows it cannot be all things to all people. Believing strongly as it does in trading resources and in alliance building, it never

wastes time in areas it doesn't understand. It sets up symbiotic relationships that achieve great things for the benefit of all participants.

6. **EMPLOYS CHALLENGING FINANCIAL, OPERATIONAL, AND CUSTOMER-PERFORMANCE MEASURES**—Seeking excellence, the SAO adopts tough performance measures that constantly challenge it, and that link successful performances to rewards.

7. **SETS STRETCH GOALS TIED TO CUSTOMER SUCCESS**—The company focused on excellence does not want its customers to ever leave. In addition to striving to achieve high customer value, it reaches beyond its assumed limits, "stretching" even higher.

8. **PROVIDES CUSTOMER RELATIONSHIP-MANAGEMENT "EDUCATION"**—Development of "soft" skills aimed at keeping customers happy is a must. Product training, technical training, and relationship skill development—the self-aligning organization provides it all!

9. **DEMONSTRATES TEAMING AND TEAM EFFECTIVENESS**— SAOs achieve their effectiveness through teams. An SAO's teaming process places customer-focused action teams and self-directed work teams at the top of the priority list.

10. **ADJUSTS, ADAPTS, AND ACTS**—The SAO develops customer-focused work processes as a matter of course as well as information systems that allow it to quickly adjust and adapt to shifting external demands. Just as importantly, the aligned organization has a bias toward action to create value at all levels.

ALIGNMENT AND PEAK PERFORMANCE

Sometimes alignment can evolve so naturally, automatically, and rapidly that an individual team's objectives merge with objectives advanced by a collaborating or even competing team. When that happens, a win-win synergy becomes absolute, functioning on an oddly transcendent, extraordinary, higher plane.

EXAMPLE: In his playing days, no one could beat Bill Russell, the Hall of Fame basketball star who, as captain, led the Boston Celtics to perennial world championships in the fifties and sixties. The formidable, versatile center set many records in points scored, rebounds, and assists, often making it all look so easy even as he tore his way toward a basket or stretched way in the air to block an opponent's shot.

But Russell was always the first to admit that he could never have done much of anything without his fellow teammates. Frequently citing a seamlessness of the Celtics of that era, he liked to credit this ability to play well together as responsible for creation of frequent states of "flow." That Russell's team could focus as a unit on common goals and implement united actions was only the beginning, this legend felt. On rare occasions, such integrated, relationship-based teamwork even extended to the other team, elevating the Boston Garden (or whatever arena were playing in) to a curious form of win-win environment that transcended the objectives of the game itself.

"Every so often a Celtic game would heat up so it became a mental game and would be magical," Russell once said, reflecting on the astonishing phenomenon. "When it happened, I could feel my level of play rise to a new level, surrounding not only me and the other Celtics but also the players on the other team, and the referees.

The game would be a white heat of competition, and yet somehow I couldn't feel competitive—which is a miracle in itself... On those five or ten occasions when the game ended on that special level, I literally did not care who had won."

ACCOUNTABILITY

Accountability—Webster's calls it "the state of being liable, or answerable." Without it, problems cannot be resolved to everyone's satisfaction, customer complaints cannot be answered, assignments will frequently not be carried out, at least as intended or hoped for. Many people say that accountability has been lost in the modern business organization. In the self-aligning organization, however, accountability is alive and well.

Though accountability only exists in relationships, it is ever the key test for any organization worth its salt. Firm-wide accountability is the hallmark of the truly aligned organization. Let's examine for a moment the primary manifestations of accountability. You'll see that some forms of accountability are stronger than others.

▲ **ONE TO ONE:**

We find the strongest accountability, for example, in one-to-one relationships. When Jack promises something to Jake, or Jill to Jo, accountability reigns. You just don't get any clearer than that. "I promise," we say, "I will do this for you." No wiggle room, no mental reservations. We feel obliged to carry this promise to fruition. Basically, we have seen the face of the person who is counting on us and that matter to us. So we're accountable!

▲ SMALL GROUPS AND TEAMS:

The next strongest form of accountability is found in small groups and teams, for much the same reason. A platoon in battle may be the best example. With a goal or enemy defined, it's one for all and all for one, a matter of life and death. We can see the faces of those who are depending on us; we know our "promises" personally. When it comes to an extreme case such as military conflict, making a promise under such circumstances further suggests we had *better* come through. If not, we all may not live to see the consequences.

▲ MANY TO MANY:

As accountability widens—to an organization or a company or country—it grows much weaker. The faces of those we promise are no longer seen. For this primary reason, the many-to-many form of relationships, although the bedrock of our companies and countries, require formalized systems of governance to ensure that individuals stay accountable.

Even with such formalization, however, many-to-many accountabilities only function effectively to the extent they are sanctioned by informal human networks. Take away a people's trust in its governmental leaders, for example, and sooner or later, one way or another, these leaders fall. Informal human networks rule.

Informal human networks, in fact, grow organically and are all about accountability "in the trenches." All along, they've been the primary strategic advantage of human evolution and the arrival of the Internet holds the potential to leverage them even greater. No wonder governments are working so hard to figure out ways to control and tax it!

A relevant quote from the Change Integration Team of Price Waterhouse in their book *The Paradox Principles,* sheds light on this truth:

"To build an organization, focus on the individual. Your employees, one by one, are the most critical components of the organization. The greatest leaders in the decade ahead will look upon the majority and see the one. Teams don't think, organizations don't act. Groups don't decide. We know that high-performance teams are not much more than a grouping of highly skilled, fully developed individuals... An organization's network of relationships is a critical component of today's business model."

The quote continues: "(A network) should not be overlooked as a source of strength and stability. The ability to deliver great value, maintain flexibility, and keep costs to a minimum is driving all of us to build a web of relationships with our customers, our suppliers, and in a few cases, even our competitors. Confederation, collaboration, or close integration with business partners is imperative; it is also a source of stability."

POWERSKILLS IN YOUR ORGANIZATION

The Price Waterhouse ideas reinforce the need for PowerSkills in today's organizations. When applied correctly in an organization, PowerSkills tap the power of accountability in service to the alignment of individual, team, and company goals. Once accepted, this thinking must be carried out, suggesting a tremendous commitment to training, practice, discipline, and nerve. But PowerSkills can provide the framework within which to succeed.

Where can you start? Look at your own organization and ask yourself how rich it currently is in PowerSkills. Use the following questions to guide your assessment process:

Positioning—PowerSkill #1

▲ Are your managers singing off the same page when they describe the company?

▲ Can your people at every level compellingly communicate your value proposition to different audiences in thirty seconds or less?

▲ Does your company have top-of-mind awareness among the leaders and influencers in your industry and customer base?

▲ Is word of mouth working for you to create a bigger-than-life image?

▲ Have you created the "buzz" factor around your company and offerings that attract the right people and opportunities?

Hunting—PowerSkill #2

▲ Is your company building relationships at the top of your industry's food chain?

▲ Does your company have the luxury of selecting from the best of an abundance of opportunities?

▲ How good is the business intelligence that your team develops?

▲ Is your firm consistently missing big opportunities?

▲ Are your sales and marketing costs outrunning performance?

▲ Are you establishing the right relationships that can provide the most leverage?

Coaching—PowerSkill #3

▲ Are your people "trusted advisors to clients" or mere problem-solvers and order-takers?

▲ Is your organization learning faster than the competition?

▲ Are you creating learning relationships with customers and suppliers?

▲ Are your business leaders creating a self-directed and empowered workforce through coaching?

▲ Have your managers discovered how to increase the speed and performance of the organization by coaching as a problem-solving, performance-improvement, and professional-development tool?

▲ Are you creating high impact, low maintenance relationships?

Leading—PowerSkill #4

▲ Does your organization lead or follow in its relationships with customers, partners and suppliers?

▲ Is there a quality of personal leadership that pervades your organization?

▲ Is a proactive "find a way or make a way" attitude part of your corporate culture?

▲ Has your leadership team established firm-wide accountability for customer-driven bottom-line results?

▲ Are you aligning your relationship resources toward your goals?

▲ Are you empowering your people to work as a team?

▲ Does your organization effectively tap the power of external relationships in order to gain competitive advantage?

▲ Is your company an industry leader that focuses upon customers or a follower that imitates competitors?

▲ Do your executives practice closed-loop delegation that produces timely results for customers?

Farming—PowerSkill #5

▲ Has your organization become easy to do business with?

▲ Have you succeeded in turning your most important customers into advocates and loyal partners?

▲ Are you leveraging the best relationships that your customers have with their most important partners?

▲ Is your organization planting the seeds of innovation and tomorrow's revenue stream with your bellwether clients?

▲ Does your organization have a stay-in-touch program that maintains communication, trust, and perceived value among customers, investors, workforce/families, suppliers, and top prospects?

THE FAST TRACK TO THE ALIGNED ORGANIZATION

After making the decision to take PowerSkills beyond your own activities and distribute them throughout your team or organization, you'll want to recruit some help with implementation. Others who have tried it can lead the way. Here are a few additional thoughts to enable you to succeed.

To be effective as a change agent capable of achieving and maintaining ongoing alignment, a business leader with overall responsibility for a business (or unit or team) needs to "own" five levers: strategy, values, structure, process, and measurement. While experience shows it's most effective for leaders to coach their organizations, it's also critical to lead. Ignore this principle and desired change will not occur.

Leaders must take ownership for the communication and implementation of these five levers. Failing to do so invites disaster. In my coaching sessions with CEOs, I sometimes ask them to prepare a three-column analysis of (1) decisions they believe they should make on their own, (2) decisions that they want to collaborate with their executive team or advisors, and (3) decisions that they want to process out and achieve with a consensus with their team as a group. Typically, they recognize the pain that they have caused themselves by trying too hard to collaborate on the five levers when what they need is input and to provide the decisions that go with their leadership position.

Too often, for example, I have observed CEOs lobbying to "get permission" from their VPs, perhaps for an organizational restructuring or to shift key executive assignments. Just as often, I've seen VPs abdicate evaluation of the CEO's ideas, transferring perhaps to the CFO who may not be qualified to carry out such an evaluation. Many CFOs, for example, are unfamiliar with organizational theory or practice or the use of balanced scorecards of qualitative and quantitative measurements. So the task may not get carried out effectively.

Another mistake many CEOs make is overly relying on reorganizations and external appointments as crude tools to "work around" the culture. This way, they avoid attempts to change it in any directed sense. Too often they focus their energies on products, strategies, or initiatives, none of which, generally speaking, will be either integrative or aligning. They may actually reinforce only firefighting or Band-Aid approaches.

Though CEOs can and should utilize collaborative processes to prepare their "battle plans" or to fact-find for an upcoming decision, top decision-makers must nonetheless "own" their change management initiatives in the final analysis. The ultimate word on strategy, organizational structure, key processes, support systems, and performance measurements must be theirs and theirs alone. Only in this manner can a chief officer or division manager offer true value as a "coach to the organization," helping it sort out priorities to align itself with, and understand why these priorities have been chosen.

Via the coaching process, executive groups (and those who serve under them) come to support the guiding daily "beliefs" that deepen a culture. CEOs, because they've been selected to do so (it's their role!), must lead the way.

TEN TIPS FOR CHANGE

There are many other ways business leaders can implement PowerSkills in their organizations and create a culture that supports accountability and alignment. Here are a few important ideas:

1. BECOME A ROLE MODEL FOR THE DESIRED BEHAVIORS. Do this and others will follow your lead. You in effect become the cultural "ideal."

2. ENGAGE IN FREQUENT CUSTOMER AND EMPLOYEE INTERACTION, including customer surveys and progress audits to drive planning. By bringing "the outside in," you keep your entire organization focused on market performance.

3. FORM CROSS-FUNCTIONAL WORKING GROUPS OF COMPANY LEADERS FOR YOUR CULTURAL COMPASS: Use Customer

Advocacy teams, Organizational Effectiveness task force, Customer Solutions teams.

4. USE QUALIFIED CONSULTANTS AND FACILITATORS TO DESIGN BREAKTHROUGH MANAGEMENT RETREATS for the purposes of intensive planning and training. Use such retreats also to enroll employees in skill development and action planning for customer-focused cultural change. Integrate your retreat efforts with the annual executive planning calendar.

5. REMEMBER THAT SELF-ALIGNING ORGANIZATIONS ARE ALL ABOUT EMBRACING CHANGE. As such, they must be aimed at creating a strong customer-value culture adaptable to rapidly changing market dynamics. True self-aligning organizations function as if driven by tribal instincts, so the successful CEO or other management/team leader will see to it to always develop and reinforce such instincts.

6. CREATE A COACHING CULTURE FOR VERTICAL ALIGNMENT. This means connecting people with strategy by creating a culture in which performance management is an ongoing activity, supported by in-depth training in coaching skills.

7. ENCOURAGE COLLABORATION TO MAINTAIN HORIZONTAL ALIGNMENT. This means connecting processes with customers by collaborating across the organization; employees to the company, business partners to customers. Strong investments in training programs and reward systems reinforce such enterprise-wide collaborative relationship-management practices.

8. STAND BY TO COACH, REASSIGN, OR UNSEAT EXECUTIVES too focused on maintaining their own turf. I've worked with over 250 CEOs and can assure you that all too often a chief executive

will try to please rather than oust organizational "terrorists," i.e., resistant personalities unwilling to accept any change. Without a succession plan, executive-development process, or aggressive recruitment function, organizations can become overly dependent on such deficient managers or line personnel, blocking or destroying the possibilities of true organizational alignment.

9. **GET DIRECTLY INVOLVED IN THE DESIGN, TESTING, AND ROLLOUT OF ALL TEAMING PROCESSES,** using each as a key opportunity to build great teams that deliver extraordinary results. At Motorola and General Electric, for example, mature teams self-direct and self-align in many ways: by managing their own budgets, by working directly with customers and vendors, by participating in planning, by setting their own goals, by doing their own hiring, and by conducting peer reviews for performance appraisals. In advanced stages of effective self-aligning organizations, manager's coach such self-directed work teams as these in order to drive them hard on such issues as cycle time and customer satisfaction.

10. **INTEGRATE RELATIONSHIP PLANNING** for key constituencies with business planning. (See Exhibit 9.2.) Determining how you will reach and create value for your stakeholders is as important as building the financial and operational model for the business.

To achieve the status, and reality, of a self-aligning organization, a company's leaders must demand, teach and distribute the full array of PowerSkills. When applied in conjunction with fully developed tribal instincts, and galvanized by informal human networks,

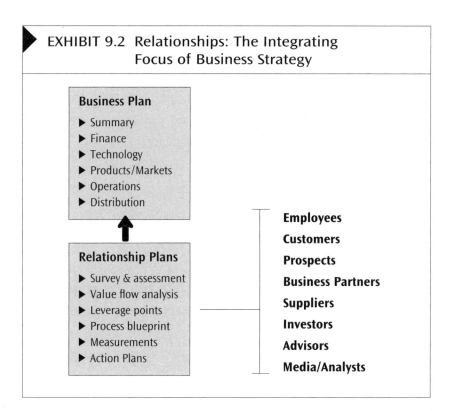

EXHIBIT 9.2 Relationships: The Integrating Focus of Business Strategy

Business Plan

▶ Summary
▶ Finance
▶ Technology
▶ Products/Markets
▶ Operations
▶ Distribution

Relationship Plans

▶ Survey & assessment
▶ Value flow analysis
▶ Leverage points
▶ Process blueprint
▶ Measurements
▶ Action Plans

Employees

Customers

Prospects

Business Partners

Suppliers

Investors

Advisors

Media/Analysts

competitive advantages take center stage. The only ingredient left is a technological toolbox to enhance these new, excellent customer-relationship functions.

In the next chapter, Technology and PowerSkills, we survey effective technology to expand the reach of our human skills. Though they shouldn't substitute for the PowerSkills themselves, many amazing technological advances now available to us can be resourced to strengthen and sustain our efforts toward positive professional change. Business leaders attuned to PowerSkills will realize, at first glance, their value.

CHAPTER KEY POINTS

▲ A coaching culture achieves vertical alignment connecting strategy with peoples' performance.

▲ A collaborative culture achieves the horizontal alignment that connects processes with customers.

▲ Creating true cultures that are in step with either strategy or systems (or both) is the right idea but may not be easy to achieve.

▲ Few organizations have developed sophisticated systems for harnessing their informal networks.

▲ Great business leaders know that alignment without distributed PowerSkills in the organization cannot be achieved.

▲ The use of PowerSkills infuses a workforce with tribal instincts that focus energies and attitudes naturally in the right directions.

▲ Firm-wide accountability is the key test for a self-aligning organization.

▲ The strongest accountability will be found in one-to-one relationships. Informal human networks grow organically and are about accountability "in the trenches."

▲ To build an organization, focus on the individual.

▲ Insist that business plans include relationship plans for each key customer and stakeholder group.

CHAPTER 10

TECHNOLOGY
AND
POWERSKILLS

"The mechanic
that would perfect
his work must first
sharpen his tools."

—Confucius

Jonathan Katz, founder of Cinnabar, a $17 million company that creates scenery and special effects for commercials, movies, and theme-park attractions, always had great faith in the powers of technology and never hesitated to say so. Early on, his company has adopted, with enthusiasm, virtually every significant communications technology of the past decade to come along, from faxes to cell phones to e-mail. "We were very attuned to the latest technologies," he told *Inc. Magazine* for a story in its February 1999 issue, "because they allowed us to stay in constant contact with our clients."

Whenever an unexpected crisis erupted—say, a budget problem or if an important prop had to be redesigned—Cinnabar employees would leap on the Internet and buzz off an e-mail or snap on a cell phone and solve the problem right then and there. By communicating to their client production companies in cyberspace they rarely had to even be with a client in the same city. They could whip out information, a question, a solution fast! Then, next moment, right back to work. An arrangement like this suggested the proverbial pot of gold—bottom-line staff and travel savings with top-of-market revenue and results. For many years under this formula, Cinnabar's revenues went up and up.

At a point, however, Katz and company began to sense trouble. Something was missing in the air; client projects had begun slowing down or going to the competition across town. When in early 1997 profits took a dramatic, unexpected dive, Katz began racking his brain trying to determine the problem.

At first, though he thought and thought and thought, no ready answers came. Then, like a streak of lightning, an "epiphany." Katz recalls: "My people had become too complacent and reliant on the conveniences of electronic communication." By this he meant faxes, e-mail, telephones. "The real heart of our business, which came out of direct contact with our clients, was not happening."

People had to occasionally "bang their heads together" in person, he realized, and e-mails and faxes did not allow this. "The virtual world," Katz explained to *Inc.*, "can lull you into thinking that it works just as well as face-to face-interaction. In fact, sometimes it doesn't work at all."

Katz then asked his people to put away all electronic gadgets and begin paying personal visits to directors, producers, and art directors at Cinnabar's client production companies. His orders were clear: *Network. Do Lunch. Circulate. Go to shoots.* As a result,

Cinnabar employees got back to basics. Technology, they rediscovered, can only support the old-fashioned face-to-face schmoozefests. Led by this "new" strategy, the company's commercial business grew 50% in the last quarter of 1998.

This anecdote may represent only the tip of the iceberg. While technophobes may rejoice to read this, my real message is: Use technology sensibly in concert with your PowerSkills. When reinforcing the Relationship Equation (relationship = trust, value and dialogue, or R = T + V + D), technology's power tools operate like magic wands. In fact, it's hard to imagine today why someone wouldn't choose to use a contact manager or personal organizer to quickly access contacts, history, tasks, and calendars. An annotated database of key relationships is a major professional and corporate asset.

But don't give the tools of technology divine rights. Use them within reason. Remember that American Express stay-in-touch dialogue mix we talked about in Chapter 8: one face-to-face meeting every year, four telephone contacts, six or more printed mailings? It must be recognized that we are human beings first, hardware jockeys second. If you leave the human touch effectively out of things, your Relationship Equation will no longer function. Trust can only be built, ultimately, between living, breathing, thinking, feeling organisms.

Here is another example from my own experience, a real turn-of-the-century story. Several years ago, after giving a talk on the importance of using an information system for managing business relationships to the AESC, The Association of Executive Search Consultants, a fellow from the audience approached me to express appreciation for what I had said.

At that time, few of the major firms in the executive recruiting industry had been using automated systems to manage their client relationships while my firm, Fenwick Partners, had become recognized as a pioneer in these methods. Competitors and industry watchers alike credited our client-server relational database for our typically high client service and fast project turnarounds. I'd been asked to come to the AESC and talk about how we had developed this system.

The search consultant, Jack, who'd come up to compliment me, had been in business for many years, and successfully. Personally, he agreed strongly with my comments on the value of having a system. He then related to me what I have since come to call "the cigar box story," a description of a relationship management system developed by his partner.

It seemed that Stanley, age 70, Jack's partner, had founded their firm in the Midwest many years back and had grown it to become a leader in filling plant manager and general manager positions for manufacturing companies. By the time of my talk, Stanley had been in the recruiting industry for over twenty-five years and was thinking of retiring. Naturally, Jack, a man of about 50, was his obvious successor.

An analytical type, Jack had spent a great deal of his time setting up a database and a report-writer on his desktop computer. These two automated systems allowed him to keep track of candidates and projects and generate printed weekly status reports to the firm's clients. Jack knew much of the firm's current success could be traced directly to clients who enjoyed the benefits of these information/communication systems.

Stanley, however, frequently expressed his disdain for computers, saying he really had "no use for them." When it came to relational database systems, Stanley had his own ideas. Over the course of his career he had perfected an effective "system" of his own, and worked like this:

Each time he won a new search assignment from a client, Stanley went out and purchased two items: a box of fine cigars and a pack of index cards. He would then go back to his office and begin working his phone. All day long he would call contact after contact in search of great candidates and leads, networking his way down his contact list. Each time he made a little progress on the assignment— speaking with a great candidate, or getting a lead on one, he would pull out a cigar from the cigar box and puff away.

Stanley also threw each index card into the box after he had entered a candidate's information with relevant notes on it. But he never filed a resume unless he'd personally interviewed a candidate and evaluated him/her as an "A" player. In this way, most candidates' information could be found by simply looking in the box.

When Stanley finally completed a search, he celebrated by smoking down the last cigar in the box (now jammed tight with candidate index cards). He'd label the box with the name of his client and project, the project's start date, and completion date. Then he'd shove the box up on a shelf in his office, usually on top of another box from a previous project, a practice he'd been following for years. By the time of my talk, Stanley's office shelves were piled high with cigar boxes, from the bottom of his credenza to his ceiling, each recalling a completed, successful search neatly labeled so he could reference it quickly in the future.

A classic schmoozer, who loved building personal relationships, Stanley's only "power tools" were his telephone, fax machine, cigar boxes, and index cards. Jocular face-to-face meetings and personal notes, letters and cards were hallmarks of Stanley's practice. Jack, on the other hand, a typically "serious" professional, diligently entered every contact into his database, focusing meticulously on the task at hand. Their clients liked them both for different reasons, acknowledging Stanley for his "people smarts" and Jack for thoroughness and professionalism.

In terms of bottom-line results, how did each approach stack up? Well, both enjoyed great reputations for completing assignments within the abysmal 175-day norm for the industry, and billing levels for both were above average for the industry. Ol' Stanley outbilled Jack, however, by about 30% year after year. It seemed his relationship management skills could not be beat, not by the most superautomated system or even by so-called professional methodologies.

Yet Jack adamantly asserted to me that day his belief that no matter how consistently superior the results from Stanley's system, the two partners couldn't grow an entire firm that way. Hearing his comment, I had to agree. "Sure," I chuckled, understanding his position. "There aren't many Stanley's out there, are there?" Jack nodded as if to say, "You got it."

Then I posed to Jack this question: What if Stanley's "high-touch" practices were combined with Jack's "high-tech" ones. Might not a true high-touch/high-tech approach pack an even greater punch? Wouldn't the new breed of consultants need some of Stanley's interpersonal instincts alongside training in the smartest uses of automated databases to deliver the very best customer service of all?

Jack liked my speculations, adding he'd been looking for such an approach for a long time. "Well, there is a way," I replied.

"We've been operating exactly this way at my firm for years." I explained that our average revenue per partner at Fenwick Partners was 10% higher than Jack and Stanley's production *combined,* and it was even possible to average closer to 105 days per project, not 175 days—firm-wide!—thereby creating yearly incomes per partner roughly double what Stanley and Jack had become accustomed to.

I suggested more: improved throughput, cycle time, client satisfaction, higher earnings for partners—all were possible for Jack and Stanley within shorter work weeks if only they merged Stanley's already-superior PowerSkills with Jack's leading-edge technology. The available array of today's technical solutions to improved communications and relationship management staggers the mind. By optimizing relationship best practices with annotated customer databases and communications technology, the payoff can be large.

WAYS NOT TO DO IT

There are so many technically supported ways for us to connect with our customers today—the Web, e-mail, paging, interactive faxes, cell phones, voice mail, video conferencing, intelligent call routing and on and on—that it's become common for misapplied technology to get in the way of building relationships. We've all endured nightmare experiences attempting to wend our way through electronic marinas in hopes of locating a knowledgeable human being empowered to solve our problem. Examples, as we know, abound. Consider this list of frustrating daily scenarios:

- ▲ "I have been trying to reach you since 9:30 a.m. Your outgoing message still has last week's holiday greeting on it and no one is picking up."

- ▲ "Sorry, I can't make an appointment with you right now. My lap top is turned off so I'm afraid I can't access my electronic calendar."

- ▲ "I tried downloading your white paper that your website describes as an interesting topic. But it never came through and instead I received a sales call."

- ▲ "Please stop sending me reminders of your specials on flower arrangements and bouquets and please take me off your mailing list. The flowers I purchased from you last year had been for my Aunt's funeral. I do know how to find you, I don't need these constant reminders."

- ▲ "We drove over an hour to be at this meeting. What do you mean you e-mailed me this morning to say it was canceled?"

- ▲ "Can you believe it? While having a design meeting with a top customer, two of our young engineering managers at the conference table kept receiving and sending each other e-mails instead of paying attention!"

- ▲ "Fred not only delivered another boring PowerPoint presentation in a darkened room to the client's top three decision-makers but he never engaged them in the dialogue."

And here's another interesting one that requires a little more explanation. One of my colleagues at a subsidiary of Emerson Electric recently found an easy way to uncover inside politics and company power relationships. Seems there was a glitch in Emerson's e-mail package such that when e-mails were blind copied, all a recipient had to do was print out the message and its distribution list of "blind" recipients would print right out too, for all the world to see! You could tell just by looking who was in the know who wasn't officially supposed to be in the know!

Suffice it to say the use of blind e-mails is a poor idea anyway—cases such as this one show it certainly does little to generate trust.

STARVING FOR KNOWLEDGE

For years Carla O'Dell, president of the American Productivity and Quality Center (APQC), based in Houston, has been studying the way major companies use information technology for the purpose of capturing best practices of effective knowledge-sharing. In spite of all our breathtaking, speedy, multifunctional technology, she reports, "We are drowning in information and starving for knowledge."

Known for the book *If Only We Knew What We Know: The Transfer of Internal Knowledge and Best Practice*, she suggests that one of the most bottom-line-driven applications of knowledge management to date has been the sharing of knowledge with customers through company websites. Put enough information about your products and services on the Web and your customers will applaud the option to solve their own problems. This saves money in salaries for large staffs of service representatives, O'Dell explains.

Knowledge sharing, in fact, may be one of the great untapped opportunities in information technology today. The ability to identify and transfer tacit knowledge, that is, the stuff between people's ears, represents "know-how" judgment, intuition, and the short cuts of how things work. Research in this area indicates that tacit knowledge may account for roughly 80% of the most valuable knowledge we possess. But due to the difficulties inherent in identifying and transferring tacit knowledge, organizations often settle for managing the 20% of explicit knowledge more easily identified, leaving the rest to chance interactions.

In the book *The Knowledge Creating Company,* Ikujiro Nonaka and Hirotaka Takeuchi offer some insights into tapping tacit knowledge. They describe innovative companies that create workspaces, organizational structures, training programs, incentives and cultures, all utilizing *both* tacit and explicit knowledge. Citing "networks of peers" and "communities of practice," they boil these bottom-line measures down to concrete ways that have been developed for improving the kinds of collaborative moments that sprout automatically in organizations rich in PowerSkills. At the end of the day, knowledge management and relationship-management systems have shown to extend both our memories and our communications.

CUSTOMER RELATIONSHIP MANAGEMENT (CRM)

Over the past several years, simple flat file databases have evolved to become the application known as contact management. Extremely powerful personal productivity tools, popular database products such as ACT and Goldmine can locate a record or name instantly, send out customized letters, faxes, and e-mails, and track project activities at the click of a mouse. No customer or contact is too small for these systems to help you find.

Companies have evolved their customer information files beyond mere billing and account histories (formerly for the sole use of a finance or sales department, for example) into robust Customer Relationship Management systems (CRMs) using such sophisticated vehicles. No longer mere mechanical record-keepers, CRMs integrate sales, service, marketing, and other professionals across the company, allowing just-in-time information, reviews of the latest products, trend-spotting and quick advancement of customer solutions. Easy ordering and problem resolution capabilities have also been designed into the best of the new systems.

It's a dream come true for many companies that have struggled for years to obtain quicker responses to customer needs from their software and management systems. The Gartner Group, an industry watchdog that tracks this software sector, has defined a "true" customer relationship management system as:

> "a business strategy aimed at understanding and anticipating the needs of an enterprise's current and potential customers. From a technological perspective, CRM involves capturing customer data from across the enterprise, consolidating all internally and externally acquired customer-related data in a central database, analyzing the consolidated data, distributing the results of that analysis to various customer touch points and using this information when dealing with customers via any touch point."

Initially the software thrust was only on billing. Then "sales force automation" came into play, then "service and marketing automation." The latest development, PRM or "partner relationship-management," recognizes the importance of managing third-party and distribution-partner relationships as well as those with customers. According to AMR Research, a Boston-based analysis firm specializing in enterprise applications, it all represents a software market projected to grow to $11.5 billion by the year 2002.

IMPROVING CUSTOMER SERVICE: THREE EXAMPLES

Until recently, industry analysts reported that failure rates for sales and service-reengineering initiatives sometimes ran as high as 70%, the biggest difficulty being the alignment of the customer-focus strategy and CRM system with the corporate culture. Usually a lack of organizational preparation and training is cited for the shortfall. As managers have recognized this, budgets for CRM training now routinely win approval along with, even prior to, the purchase of a new system.

Companies in both high- and low-technology fields now use information technology to improve their customer service. Fueled by changes in thinking about the power of managing relationships more proactively, most Global 2000 companies have in fact undergone several generations of CRMs. The effort is always there to keep abreast of the most effective ones. Consider the following examples:

EXAMPLE #1: WASTE MANAGEMENT, INC., ONE CENTRALIZED KNOWLEDGE-BASE

The world's leading provider of waste management services, Waste Management, Inc.'s revenues in 1996 were $9.2 billion. Through its many subsidiaries, WMI provides integrated solid and hazardous waste services in 23 countries. But its IT Support Center, managing the company's workload for many years with an outdated information system, routinely handed data right over to analysts, losing track, in the process, of problem resolutions.

Also, every time a customer called, the company rep had to spend time doing research on a problem and then call the customer back. Result: lengthy resolution times, inconsistent support. By all accounts, WMI needed a whole new system if it desired a stronger organization and a competitive advantage.

During a major reengineering effort within the company, 16 support groups, using different processes and reporting methods, were consolidated into a single support group with specialized teams. This plan included *one* centralized knowledge database organized from multiple sources to improve information sharing throughout all of the company's teams. Partnering with a leading software vendor to standardize their internal support center, Waste Management, Inc. created a central Support Center staffed with one hundred analysts providing technical support to more than 56,000 employees.

Today these employees access a wide range of information technology—financial software applications, truck dispatching systems, mainframes, desktops. The WMI IT Support and Field Support Center averages 25,000 service and support calls each month from employees at hundreds of working locations throughout the United States.

Given the volume of calls that this megasupport division receives, and the range of technologies utilized, WMI requires a robust infrastructure for its centralized knowledge database. The new set-up has therefore been configured to allow tracking and managing of all employee support requests and collection of valuable feedback so that in-house developers may further customize applications. Future plans call for such employee self-service options as enabling callers to resolve issues themselves technologically, i.e., without the assistance of a support representative.

EXAMPLE #2: HEWLETT-PACKARD, MINIMIZING REDUNDANCY

Successful businesses like Hewlett-Packard's Products Support Division (PSD), which supports HP's printer, fax, PC, and handheld product lines, have a common problem: As a customer base expands, internally developed support systems begin to reveal their limitations. Until recently, their customer-service representatives (CSR) did not have a way of tracking the progress of a customer's issue even after repeated calls to and from the customer. Nor could CSRs look back at a previous customer's record in which a similar issue had been raised and learn what have been done before. In addition, valuable customer feedback on products company-wide could not be easily shared department to department.

But as a recognized leader in customer-service and support, HP required all those features—and more—from its support system, so they selected a leading CRM software solutions provider and created a system with the desired levels of quality, accuracy, and consistency of response.

Currently, 1,500 PSD customer service reps use the CRM system, with records of results showing that 85 percent of customer issues now are resolved quickly and accurately on the first call. In addition to automating call tracking, problem resolution, and service and support management, HP reports that the new system also allows the company to minimize redundant support efforts while significantly increasing staff productivity and simultaneously decreasing labor costs.

With such excellence in customer asset-management in place, HP can for the first time in its history maintain a comprehensive information database of both customers and products, from product information such as specifications, benefits, and warranties, to problem resolutions and predictive alerts. Among those accessing this information are the product development, manufacturing, and quality assurance departments of each HP product line currently supported by PSD. Such departments use the available data to refine their products in order to keep enhancing customer satisfaction and loyalty.

EXAMPLE #3: CARDIORESPONSE, MANAGING A COMPLEX HUB

Heart patients are customers too! CardioResponse, a 24-hour telecare center for people with heart disease, tracks medical profiles and manages a complex communications hub touching patients, medical professionals, and ambulance services. With a new software system, patients can give and get their EKG readings over the telephone as well as update their records and instantaneously contact health-care professionals. Via simple paging mechanisms, an ambulance can be dispatched at once over an integrated telephone system.

"Relationships define the modern sales process, and the fundamental building blocks of these relationships are the same in both the personal and business realms," Danna Voth, a writer for *Sales and Field Force Automation Magazine* explains, citing such building blocks as empathy, communication, commitment, sharing, intuition, flexibility, and multitasking. The last three, she feels, are particularly enabled by technological connectivity.

TIME FOR A BALANCED OPERATING SYSTEM FOR YOUR BUSINESS?

Anyone with a desktop computer knows by now what's meant by the term "operating system." The way a computer starts, runs, and maintains all its various functions and devices in a mission to store, access, and process information is a fair definition of the term. Traditionally thought of as a software "traffic cop," your computer's operating system basically makes your hardware components do something worthwhile.

Consequently, your company's successful operating system must also take into account many elements if it is to perform well. These include the know-how to modify instructions, interconnectivity, security, low overhead, an ability to operate with both client and server, the capability to operate individually as well as in a network, ease of operability, seamlessness, cost effectiveness, and the capacity to enable multitasking. The human network and the computer network have similar issues.

To many business leaders, it's becoming more and more clear that for a company to run effectively and stay in alignment, the computer operating-system metaphor is useful. When you establish within your company, for example, customer-focused strategies, systems, and culture, as we have advised throughout this book, you are ensuring that you've installed a good company operating system.

Are you steadily drawing customers to the center of your business? It's a good question to ask if you wish to create a total organizational response as your way of doing business with your customers. This is another way of describing your "operating system," designed to consistently and naturally build value for your customers as well as for other high-level constituencies of your enterprise.

A good company operating system (way of doing business) thus consists of six principle elements:

1. The way in which your organization communicates its value (or its many values) to its market and its industry.

2. The manner in which your organization attracts, develops, and retains customers and talented employees.

3. The shape by which your organizational objectives align with that of your employees, extended workforce, and suppliers.

4. The manner in which your teams collaborate to create maximum customer value.

5. The way your organization gathers business intelligence and seizes opportunity.

6. The way your top-level partnerships and alliances contribute to your bottom-line.

Throughout all these elements runs a common, but critical, thread: Who in your organization touches your customers? Probably, if you think about it thoroughly, you'll conclude everybody does! When PowerSkills are adopted and practiced company-wide, you ensure as well that your overall operating system really hums.

What about results? We might list the "results measures" of your organization's operating system this way:

▲ revenue growth per employee

▲ traditional performance measures: Return on Investment (ROI), Earnings per Share (EPS)

▲ time to market

▲ customer and employee satisfaction

▲ share of customer

▲ level of brand loyalty

▲ retention

▲ relationship quality

The integrated approach to business views value-creation through the lens of business interrelationships inside and out. This means great relationship management at the company, team, and professional level. Without an operating system properly designed, tested, networked, and fully deployed, corporate-wide performance will ultimately suffer.

In my experience, operating systems at most businesses have been out of date for a long time. Most continually fail to deploy the full resources of the organization. The only solution I know is to build a replacement system on the realities of the new distributed workplace.

Without a behavior-oriented operating system that builds profitable relationships, no software solutions to either CRM (Customer Relationship Management) or TQM (Total Quality Management), or any other hopeful acronym will succeed. Only by dealing directly with the best practices of relationship management at all levels can we achieve the dream of top-level performance with bottom-line results. What's required are fully customer intimate, self-renewing organizations that are quick to respond when faced with dramatic, sudden swings of consumer demand. In this maddening, turn-on-a-dime age, nothing less will do.

Training programs that are not strategic; software that ignores cultural adoption; process programs without direct, swift connections to key business constituencies—all such weaknesses contribute to failure and business breakdown each and every time. Technology without PowerSkills does not make for a successful operating environment and neither will it produce the kind of employee/customer satisfaction mirror that can deliver high service from a human-friendly workplace.

Only well-thought-out, dedicated, pervasive combinations of high-tech/high-touch can give the desired results.

Note: Our PowerSkills.com website is continually updated with links to information about the latest technology applications for advancing business relationships and workplace productivity. Click on our site whenever you wish to update your understanding of what's currently available in this area.

CHAPTER KEY POINTS

▲ When we optimize relationship best practices by merging them with automated tools, the bottom-line payoff can be large.

▲ Knowledge sharing may be one of the great untapped opportunities in information technology today.

▲ Knowledge management and relationship management, when hand-in-hand with computer and software systems, have been shown to extend both our memories and our communications.

▲ "True" customer relationship management systems are business strategies aimed at understanding and anticipating the needs of current and potential customers.

▲ Throughout all the elements of a good organizational operating system runs a common, but critical, thread: extraordinary customer value requires a total organizational response.

▲ An integrated approach to business views value-creation through the lens of business interrelationships inside and out.

▲ Only by dealing directly with the best practices of relationship management at all levels can we achieve the dream of top-level performance with bottom-line results

RESOURCES

Click on **www.powerskills.com/technology**.

The One to One Enterprise: Tools for Competing in the Interactive Age by Don Peppers and Martha Rogers, Ph.D. New York: Currency Doubleday: 1997. ISBN 0-385-48205-1

EPILOGUE

THE ALL TERRAIN PROFESSIONAL

Today's effective business leader functions more like a high-end sports utility vehicle (SUV) than a luxury sedan or sports car,—able to perform smartly in a variety of situations with confidence, power, and flexibility. While the terrain may vary from the boardroom to the customer site, the research laboratory to the factory or distributor, from business partner to supplier, industry forum, or cyberspace, the evolved professional must adapt quickly to seize opportunities. Tomorrow's leaders are training to be what I call the "all terrain professional" (ATP)—entrepreneurial, highly collaborative, multi-tasking, and increasingly autonomous.

The shape of business models and markets are changing swiftly and the antidote for these sweeping changes is to effectively manage relationships on many levels, on any terrain. ATPs stay engaged with their networks inside and outside the company and get traction at every turn to constantly stay in tune with the competitive landscape. Like an SUV, the All Terrain Professional is a generalist who has evolved quite rapidly in the past decade and understands how to leverage the expertise of others in both loose and tight organizational connections. So often today, there is no staff of on-board experts to help figure things out. To get things done in Internet speed means collaboration and the use of technology whenever and wherever it makes sense.

What's become increasingly clear is that professionals in the workforce must think and act like entrepreneurs even though many individuals will still resist this idea. There's simply no place to hide in today's high performance organization. No longer can any of us assume that we will experience only one or even two careers over the course of a work lifetime: five is now the predicted norm, and more for the most versatile or adventurous among us.

This new work world dynamic has had the effect of pushing us all, as our experience grows, in the direction of ever-increasing personal autonomy. Yet, ironically, we must learn to collaborate to truly achieve it. Today our value is found in thinking like a general manager or a consultant concerned with the *what* and *when* of things as opposed to merely the *how*. While we focus on our core competencies and partner with others to deliver full solutions, we also strive to keep the Big Picture in mind in our endeavor to create a new order of things. That is what entrepreneurs do. Within such a brave new world, PowerSkills enable us to take quick advantage of both the transitions and the opportunities, recognizing that such fast action is no longer optional but a total necessity.

American style capitalism has begun to foster never-before opportunities on the Internet: do-it-yourself stock trading, global electronic commerce, self-publishing, distance learning, on-line research, to name just a few. Well-developed mechanisms now exist to support budding entrepreneurs wishing to raise capital and resources for new businesses and for "intrapreneurs" too seeking to initiate major projects within their larger organization. University entrepreneurship programs and venture forums, for example, and new financing sources, eagerly seek talented people with great ideas whom they can help.

Business leaders understand the clear value resulting from a strong focus. Without this critical ingredient, it's near impossible to build a consistently profitable business because, at the end of the day, it's the repetition of perfected solutions, and the creative reuse of work products, that allow enterprises to become predictable and efficient. But one word of caution: an intense focus over time can also become a trap, especially when it has done its job, i.e., keeping a business on track. The track may become a professional dead end.

When we only remain comfortable with what we know, we can become closed to the changing world of possibilities. Whenever successful professionals face up to the financial or professional risks of a new endeavor, weighing them against the need for personal creative expression, fear of failing holds the power to do them in. Though *focus, focus, focus* may in general be good advice for a business, it can also starve the soul of the very best business leaders and owners. Learning curves have a tendency to flatten out, so that professionals who wish to keep growing must think like Captain Kirk and Ulysses, "boldly going where no one (or you!) has ever gone before." Do otherwise and risk stagnation, and loss of momentum, at the very least.

When truly dedicated to life long learning, we must re-pot ourselves every so often so that our roots and branches can grow rapidly again. To remain self-directed, we must from time to time take career choices and transitions into our own hands in this rapidly changing world. Otherwise, mediocrity, boredom, underemployment and obsolescence show up on our doorstep. Growing through this cycle of dependence to independence to interdependence, we begin recognizing the natural interconnnected-ness of our world. Relationships built years earlier have a tendency to pay us back in unexpected dividends. Such pleasant surprises almost always are traceable to a particular value we provided others long ago. My own career serves as an example.

After retiring from the executive recruiting industry and selling my ownership in a leading firm, I decided once again to "take the plunge" and strike out in a very new direction. My first step involved a mid-career sabbatical. Traveling widely, I spent many of my sojourns informally scouting for new ideas, talking to people, asking them how they did things, what they believed in. This extremely beneficial process reinvigorated me with a fresh energy which I was going to need when I got back home to tackle the next phase of my life and work.

When that time came, I went about initiating several new career thrusts simultaneously. Having built many strategic relationships over 25 years, and now having some risk capital, I decided to become a private investor and advisor to early stage technology companies. This often involves such skills as coaching CEOs, forming boards, and facilitating executive planning retreats. Fortunately sizing up business problems was a strength of mine. I also knew how it felt to be in the hot seat, so helping others who struggled to improve their own top-level performances, and in turn, their companies' performances, rounded out my career ambitions. Blending investing and advising was something I had always wanted to do, although at first I didn't quite know how I would get started.

Then I began thinking about how I might rekindle my writing skills, publish some articles and a book. I enjoy public speaking and considered converting my lessons learned in business into an executive seminar and change management company.

When I reviewed all my new objectives, I realized that I was attempting to master several new areas—investing, serving as a Director, CEO coaching, writing, and public speaking. To succeed, I needed to connect with people who were better than me in these areas, who knew more, who could teach me, who could help me grow. My existing VIRs became my guides.

Becoming a writer meant getting to know publishers and editors, how they work, what they want, and what I could do for them. It also meant starting out with published articles in the trade press and moving on eventually to this book. After many years of private research and scribbling, I greatly desired to make that process more concrete. Sharing my message as a keynote speaker required practicing public speaking, attending speaker conferences to educate myself in that arena. Fortunately, I found some great coaches and mentors, articles, and books to read, and got lots of feedback to act on.

Becoming a sought-after CEO coach meant extending myself beyond knowing what it takes and feels to be an organization's leader to developing coaching skills and learning techniques and inventing a few of my own that would be suitable for challenging top executives. Of course, these endeavors also meant getting the word out by identifying, calibrating and profiling my Nifty Fifty as well as my larger relationship web. But you know all that already!

EAGLES AND ANGELS

Regarding my goal to become a private investor and advisor to young high technology companies, I expressed my interest one day to a successful former client of mine and former chief executive, Tony Helies. I knew that Tony had gotten very active in "angel investing" in which investors with a minimum of a million dollars in investable funds, become personally involved in mentoring early-stage companies, and in the writing and development of their business plans. Angel investors also help with key management selections and take substantial risks of their time and money on deals generally at too early a stage for institutional venture capitalists. Certainly no bank would ever finance companies such as these, hence the term "angel" developed to denote an investor willing to help out otherwise-dismissed entrepreneurs needing assistance in getting their business ideas and dreams off the ground.

Angel investors typically have lots of personal operating experience from their own careers to share with a new company. Because of their extensive network of VIRs, they can also open many large doors and arrange market trials and product launches.

After some evaluation, Tony and the others in this new investment "group," Walnut Venture Associates, many of whose members I'd developed good relationships with over the years, officially invited me to become a charter member.

Walnut Venture Associates is composed of fifteen Boston-area entrepreneurs/ investors who have joined forces to fund and aid the development of local companies through their collective business experience and contacts. Taken together, individuals in the group have founded twelve companies, served as the CEO of more than fifteen companies, have invested in over one-hundred and fifty private companies, and have sat on Board of Directors of over fifty companies. Their skills include seasoned depth in all functional areas including general management, marketing, sales, product development, marketing communications, and finance.

Frequently Walnut Venture Associates partners with other venture firms and angel networks to share opportunities and finance larger deals. Through partnering, we have been able to leverage small investments as individual investors with a highly experienced network. The multiplier effect of associating with my fascinating Walnut friends, strong individuals with many interests, deep knowledge and wisdom, has been utterly amazing. This self-aligning "organization" runs the gamut from evaluating business plans to conducting due diligence to arranging and finalizing financing and building teams. Its combination of well-honed skills and established relationship webs, developed by these All Terrain Professionals over their lifetimes, demonstrates phenomenal results time and time again.

I decided to close this book with my reflections on Walnut Venture Associates because to me each of my eagle/angel Walnut colleagues shines a living testament to the superiority of PowerSkills in action. Having observed the positioning, hunting, coaching, leading and farming practices of these outstanding leaders, I can attest to the benefits of their results-oriented, relationship-based approach. I am also pleased to see the time and money that they individually donate to local charities. If there be any doubt in your mind at this point as to what might be gained by adopting the five PowerSkills, just cast a glance at the proven senior executives in your own community who have dedicated themselves to a similar brand of mentoring, investing and philanthropy.

Now it's time for you to fast-forward your own career by visualizing and actualizing your own brand of PowerSkills. As you do, I invite you to open yourself to the possibilities. Undoubtedly you will go farther than you may have ever imagined while you construct new, value-based top-level relationships with increasing bottom-line results.

Go boldly forth now and make it so.

WEBSITE

www.powerskills.com

Our website contains resources and links to help you implement the concepts in this book. It is continually updated to provide you with the latest information for advancing business relationships, so visit us often. You will find information on:

- ▲ easy book ordering methods for any quantity
- ▲ speaking engagements
- ▲ company training

We welcome your comments, input, lessons learned, suggestions and critiques.

BIBLIOGRAPHY

Albrecht, Karl, *The Only Thing That Matters: Bringing the Power of the Customer into the Center of Your Business.* New York, NY: Harper Business, 1992. ISBN 0-88730-639-X

Albrecht, Karl, and Zemke, Ron, *Service America: Doing Business in the New Economy.* New York: Warner Books, 1995. ISBN 0-44639-092-5

Baker, Wayne E., *Networking Smart: How to Build Relationships for Personal and Organizational Success.* New York: McGraw-Hill Inc., 1994. ISBN 0-07-005092-9

Bayan, Richard, *Words That Sell: The Thesaurus to Help You Promote Your Products, Services, and Ideas.* Chicago: Contemporary Books, 1984. ISBN: 0-8092-4799-2

Beckwith, Harry, *Selling the Invisible: A Field Guide to Modern Marketing.* New York: Warner Books, 1997. ISBN 0-446-52094-2

Bell, Chip R., *Customers as Partners: Building Relationships That Last.* San Francisco: Berrett-Koehler Publishers, Inc., 1994. ISBN 1-881052-54-0

Bennis, Warren, *On Becoming a Leader.* Perseus Press, 1994. ISBN 0-201-409291

Bennis, Warren, *Organizing Genius: The Secrets of Creative Collaboration.* Reading, MA: Addison Wesley, 1997. ISBN 0-201-33989-7

Bosworth, Michael T., *Solution Selling: Creating Buyers in Difficult Selling Markets*. Burr Ridge, IL: Irwin Professional Publishing, 1995. ISBN 0 7863-0315-8

Bower, Martin, *The Will to Lead: Running a Business with a Network of Leaders*. Boston: Harvard Business School Publishing, 1997. ISBN 0-875-84758-7

Brandenburger, Adam M., and Nalebuff, Barry, J., *Co-opetition*. New York, DoubleDay, 1996. ISBN 0-385-47949-2

Burley-Allen, Madelyn, *Listening: The Forgotten Skill*. New York, NY: John Wiley & Sons, Inc., 1995. ISBN 0-471-01587-3

Carkhuff, Robert R., *The Development of Human Resources: Education, Psychology, and Social Change*. Holt, Rinehart and Winston, Inc., 1971. ASIN 0030846986

Chopra, Deepak, *The Seven Spiritual Laws of Success: A Practical Guide to the Fulfillment of Your Dreams*. San Rafael, CA: Amber-Allen Publishing and New World Library, 1994. ISBN 1-878424-11-4

Covey, Stephen R., *Principle-Centered Leadership*. New York: Simon & Schuster, 1992. ISBN 0-671-74910-2

Cross, Richard, and Smith, Janet, *Customer Bonding: Pathway to Lasting Customer Loyalty*. Lincolnwood, IL: NTC Business Books, 1995. ISBN 0-8442-3318-8

Csikszentmihalyi, Mihaly, *Flow: The Psychology of Optimal Experience*. New York: HarperCollins Publishers, 1990. ISBN: 0-06-092043-2

Dreher, Diane, *The Tao of Personal Leadership*. New York, HarperCollins Publishers , Inc., 1996. ISBN: 0-88730-837-6

Frank, Milo O., *How to Get Your Point Across in 30 Seconds or Less*. London, Corgi Books, 1986. ISBN 0-671-72752-4

Goldratt, Eliyahu M., *The Goal.* Croton-on-Hudson: North River Press, 1992. ISBN 0-88427-061-0

Goleman, Daniel, *Emotional Intelligence.* New York: Bantam Books, 1995, 1997. ISBN 0-553-37506-7

Gracián, Baltasar, *The Art of Worldly Wisdom.* New York: Doubleday, 1992. ISBN 0-385-42131-1

Hargrove, Robert, *Masterful Coaching.* San Francisco: Jossey-Bass Pfeiffer Printing, 1995. ISBN: 0-89384-281-8

Hill, Sam, and Rifkin, Glenn, *Radical Marketing.* New York: Harperbusiness, 1999. ISBN 0-887-30905-4

Hughes, Arthur M., *Strategic Database Marketing.* Chicago, IL: Probus Publishing Company, 1994. ISBN 1-55738-551-3

Katzenbach, Jon, *Teams at the Top: Developing Teams and Individual Leaders.* Boston: Harvard Business School, 1997. ISBN 0-87584-789-7

Kinlaw, Dennis C., *Coaching for Commitment: Managerial Strategies for Obtaining Superior Performance.* San Francisco: Jossey-Bass/Pfeiffer Printing, 1989. ISBN: 0-88390-227-3

Kotter, John P., *Power and Influence: Beyond Formal Authority.* New York: The Free Press, A Division of Macmillan, Inc., 1985. ISBN 0-02-918330-8

Labovitz, George, and Rosansky, Victor, *The Power of Alignment: How Great Companies Stay Centered and Accomplish Extraordinary Things.* New York: John Wiley & Sons, 1997. ISBN 0-47117-790-3

Landsberg, Max, *The Tao of Coaching: Boost Your Effectiveness at Work by Inspiring Those Around You.* Santa Monica, CA: Knowledge Exchange, LLC, 1997. ISBN 1-888232-34-X

Lau-tzu, *TAO Te Ching* (Translation by Mitchell, Steven). Harper Perennial, 1992. ISBN 0-06-081245-I

Lengioni, Patrick, *The Five Temptations of a CEO.* New York: Simon & Schuster Audio, 1998. Tape 04335-8

Leonard, George, *Mastery: The Keys to Success and Long-Term Fulfillment.* New York: Penguin Group, 1991. ASIN: 0453007546

Levitt, Theodore, *After the Sale is Over.* Boston: Harvard Business Review Article, September 1993

Lynch, Robert Porter, *Business Alliances Guide: The Hidden Competitive Weapon.* New York; John Wiley & Sons, Inc., 1993. ISBN 0-471-57030-3

Mackay, Harvey, *Dig Your Well Before You're Thirsty.* New York: Doubleday, 1997. ISBN 0-385-48543-3

McCall, Jr., Morgan, *High Flyers: Developing the Next Generation of Leaders.* Boston: Harvard Business School Press, 1998. ISBN 0-87584-336-0

McKenna, Regis, *Real Time: Preparing for the Age of the Never Satisfied Customer.* 1997. ISBN 0-87584-794-3

McKenna, Regis, *Relationship Marketing: Successful Strategies for the Age of the Customer.* Addison-Wesley, 1991. ISBN 0-201-62240-8

Mintzberg, Henry, *The Rise and Fall of Strategic Planning.* New York: The Free Press, 1994. ISBN 0-02-921605-2

Moore, Geoffrey, *Crossing the Chasm.* New York: HarperBusiness, 1991. ISBN 0-06-662002-3

Moore, James F., *The Death of Competition: Leadership and Strategy in the Age of Business Ecosystems.* New York: Harperbusiness, 1997. ISBN 0-887-30850-3

Musgrave, James, and Anniss, Michael, *Relationship Dynamics.* New York: The Free Press, 1996. ISBN 0-684-82449-3

Naisbitt, John, and Aburdene, Patricia, *Megatrends 2000.* New York: Harper Publishing, 1982. ISBN 0-380-70437-4

Naisbitt, John, *Global Paradox.* New York: Avon Books, 1995. ISBN 0-380-72489-8

National Association of Corporate Directors, *Report of the NACD Blue Ribbon Commission on Performance Evaluation of Chief Executive Officers, Boards, and Directors.* Washington, D.C., 1995.

Nonaka, Ikujiro, Takeuchi, Hirotaka, and Takeuchi, Hiro, *The Knowledge-Creating Company: How Japanese Companies Create the Dynamics of Innovation.* Oxford University Press, 1995. ISBN 0-195-09269-4

O'Dell, Carla, Essaides, Nilly, Ostro, Nilly, *If Only We Knew What We Know: The Transfer of Internal Knowledge and Best Practice.* New York: The Free Press, A Division of Macmillan, Inc., 1998. ISBN 0-684-4474-5

Palmer, Helen, *The Enneagram in Love & Work.* San Francisco, CA: HarperSanFrancisco, 1995. ISBN 0-06-250679-x

Pearce, Herb, *The Enneagram in Organization.* Arlington, MA, 1996.

Peoples, David A. *Selling to the Top.* New York: John Wiley & Sons, Inc., 1993. ISBN: 0-471-58104-6

Peppers, Don, and Rogers, Martha, Ph.D., *The One to One Future: Building Relationships One Customer at a Time.* New York: Bantam Doubleday Dell Pub, 1997. ISBN 0-385-48566-2

Peppers, Don, and Rogers, Ph.D., Martha., *The One to One Enterprise: Tools for Competing in the Interactive Age.* New York: Currency Doubleday: 1997. ISBN 0-385-48205-1

Peters, Thomas, and Waterman, Robert H., *In Search of Excellence: Lessons from America's Best-Run Companies.* New York: Warner Books, 1988. ISBN 0-446-38507-7

Peters, Tom, *The Brand Called You.* Fast Company Magazine, October:November 1997.

Price Waterhouse, Change Integration Team, *The Paradox Principles: How High-Performance Companies Manage Chaos, Complexity, and Contradiction to Achieve Superior Results.* Price Waterhouse, 1996. ISBN 0-7863-0499-5

Reichheld, Frederick F., *The Loyalty Effect: The Hidden Force Behind Growth, Profits, and Lasting Value.* Boston, MA: Harvard Business School Press, 1996. ISBN 0-87584-448-0

Ries, Al, and Trout, Jack, *The 22 Immutable Laws of Marketing.* New York, HarperCollins Publishers, 1993. ISBN 0-88730-666-7

Ricchiuto, Jack, *Collaborative Creativity: Unleasing the Power of Shared Thinking.* Oak Hill Press, 1997. ISBN 1-886-93912-8

Riso, Don Richard, *Understanding the Enneagram: The Practical Guide to Personality Types.* Boston: Houghton Mifflin Company, 1990. ISBN 0-395-52026-6 and 0-395-52148-3

Robbins, Anthony, *Awakening the Giant Within: How to Take Immediate Control of Your Mental, Emotional, Physical & Financial Destiny!* Fireside, 1993. ISBN 0-671-79154-0

Schrage, Michael, *No More Teams! Mastering the Dynamics of Creative Collaboration.* New York: Currency-DoubleDay, 1995. (Originally published in 1989 as Shared Minds.) ISBN 0-385-47603-5

Shaker, Steven M., and Gembicki, Mark P., *The WarRoom Guide to Competitive Intelligence.* New York: McGraw-Hill, 1999. ISBN 0-07-058057-X

Stanley, Dr. Thomas J., *Networking with the Affluent and Their Advisors.* Burr Ridge, IL: Irwin Professional Publishing, 1993. ISBN 1-55623-891-6

Tenner, Edward, *Why Things Bite Back: Technology and the Revenge of Unintended Consequences.* New York: Alfred A. Knopf, 1996. ISBN 0-679-42563-2

Tieger, Paul D., and Barron-Tieger, Barbara, *The Art of SpeedReading People.* New York: Little Brown & Company, 1998. ISBN: 0-316-84525-6

Trout, Jack, with Rivkin, Steve, *The New Positioning: The Latest on the World's #1 Business Strategy.* New York, McGraw-Hill Book Company, 1996. ISBN 0-07-065328-3

Vavra, Terry G, *After-Marketing: How to Keep Customers for Life Through Relationship Marketing.* Burr Ridge, Ill: Irwin Professional Publishing, 1992. ISBN 0-78630405-7

Waldroop, James, and Butler, Timothy, *The Executive As Coach.* Boston: Harvard Business Review, November—December 1996.

Weiss, Alan, *Million Dollar Consulting: The Professional's Guide to Growing a Practice.* R.R. Donnelley & Sons Company, 1992. ISBN 0-07-069284-9

Whitney, John O., *The Trust Factor: Liberating Profits & Restoring Corporate Vitality.* New York: McGraw-Hill Inc., 1996. ISBN 0-07-070017-6

Wiersema, Fred, *Customer Intimacy.* Santa Monica, CA: Knowledge Exchange, 1996. ISBN 1-888-23200-5

Williams, Virginia, Ph.D., and Williams, Redford, M.D., *Lifeskills.* New York: Times Books, 1997. ISBN: 0-8129-2424-X

ACKNOWLEDGMENTS

First, I would like to acknowledge the three people who have most made this project possible:

My wife Judi, my life partner, project manager extraordinaire, critical thinker, and inspiring muse.

Ken Lizotte, my writing coach and editorial consultant who dedicated his unique combination of expertise, creativity, and humor to this project.

Hal Shear, Chairman of the National Association of Corporate Directors of New England and advisor to many companies, for his many contributions of insight, encouragement, and support.

In addition, two business colleagues in particular deserve special recognition for helping this project evolve and for assisting me in the dissection and dissemination of its body of knowledge: Russ Manthy, course development expert, who helped turn my initial seminar workbook and developing ideas into a fully professional training program with a leaders' guide now enjoyed by major corporations and Jim Blaschke, who worked tirelessly to perfect the delivery of relationship management, company training, and consulting programs.

I'd also like to recognize Charley Polachi and Hale Cochran, my former partners and PowerSkills masters at Fenwick Partners (now a unit of Heidrick and Struggles). Both of these impressive professionals helped me build an extremely successful service business based entirely around high-value relationships.

Finally, it would be impossible for me to recount here all of the many other executives, entrepreneurs, colleagues, and clients I have known over the years who have generously discussed and debated ideas contained in this book with me, and who have proven themselves to be sterling examples of PowerSkills in action. They should know that, for all their help to me and for the great enthusiasm they have shown for work and life, I am deeply honored to have known them and eternally grateful for their support.

ABOUT THE AUTHOR

James Masciarelli is an entrepreneur, private investor, and CEO coach. He has dedicated his professional life to coaching leaders and building executive teams. He has founded and grown several companies as CEO.

Jim has served as an executive consultant to a wide mix of industry leaders including: Advanced Technology Laboratories, Apple Computer, Cisco Systems, Citrix Systems, Compaq Computer, Digital Telecommunications Inc., Dynatech, Eastman Kodak, FirstSense Software, Geo-Tel Communications, IBM, Lotus Development, MicroE, Millipore, Sequent Computer, Stratus Computer, Video Server, Wildfire Communications, and XEVO.

As a Principal of Walnut Venture Associates he advises and invests in emerging growth information-technology companies in the Northeast.

Jim is a board member of the National Association of Corporate Directors of New England and serves as a director and executive advisory board member to several private companies.

Dedicated to lifelong learning, Jim has made contributions in several fields. In the early seventies, as Executive Director of an urban agency, he pioneered a new approach to psychotherapy and counseling for adolescents. His interests then shifted to human resource management in the electronics and computer industry, where he spent several years as Director of North American Human Resources for Data General during its explosive growth years.

In the eighties, Jim co-founded Fenwick Partners, a high-technology retained executive search firm for which he became nationally recognized and was featured in the book, *The Career Makers*. As CEO, Jim grew the firm over eleven years to a national practice with international affiliates. Fenwick Partners is now part of the global executive search firm, Heidrick and Struggles.

Jim earned an A.B. in Psychology at Holy Cross College, an MBA at Babson College, and did postgraduate work in clinical psychology. A skillful public speaker, he is author of nationally published articles and is a guest lecturer at MIT and Harvard Business School.